Your Best Friend

Our Precious Privilege:
A Personal Friendship
with Jesus Christ!

Your Best Friend

Lottie Beth Hobbs

HARVEST PUBLICATIONS
P.O. Box 8456
Fort Worth, Texas 76124

Other Books by Lottie Beth Hobbs

Victory Over Trials —
Encouragement from the Life of Job

Choosing Life's Best —
The Practical Plan of Proverbs

Daughters of Eve —
Strength for Today from Women of Yesterday

You Can Be Beautiful —
With Beauty That Never Fades

If You Would See Good Days —
Help for Daily Decisions

Your Best Friend
ISBN 0-913838-11-X

10th English Printing

Cover art by Peggy Hobbs

Copyright 1969 by Harvest Publications
Fort Worth, Texas 76124

Contents

Your Best Friend

SUPPOSE you were expecting Jesus to visit your home to-
night, to dine at your table, and to talk with your family.
Can you visualize how you would feel? What anticipation!
What careful preparation! What an exalted privilege!

Mary and Martha had this glorious opportunity. Jesus had
no earthly home. But when humanity's problems pressed
heavily upon his heart, and when his body was weary and
worn from dusty travels and jostling multitudes, one place of
refuge was the home of Mary and Martha and their brother
Lazarus. There he could be sure of a warm welcome, understanding hearts, and physical sustenance to revive his tired
body. These dear friends lived in Bethany, a little village
nestled on the eastern slope of Mount Olivet near Jerusalem.
They must have been wonderful people, for Jesus loved them
dearly (Jno. 11:5,36). In them our Lord evidently found a
common bond and communion of the spirit. Surely this be-
speaks the highest praise.

Mary and Martha! How many little girls even to this day
are given these names — for the very words carry a connota-
tion of beauty and purity and strength which parents would
desire their daughters to emulate. Some of the most heart-
warming of all sacred scenes include these two lovely women.
This has placed them among the most beloved and popular
people of all time. All women can picture the mood which
must have pervaded their home as it buzzed with activity in
preparation for their Guest. Though Christ probably visited
often, we cannot imagine that such times became common-

place for them, because every recorded account clearly shows that he occupied an exalted place of honor in their hearts.

How thrilled we would be if Jesus came to our home. This is what we are prone to think. But do we really mean it? Since we cannot entertain him physically, we sometimes forget that actually he either dwells as a guest in our hearts and homes, or else we have closed the door against him.

He is our Best Friend. He loved us enough to die for us. He wants to be a close personal friend, for he said: "Behold, I stand at the door, and knock: if any man hear my voice, and open the door, I will come in to him, and will sup with him, and he with me" (Rev. 3:20).

The question is: are we his friends? Real friendship is reciprocal. Do we return the friendship of One who is willing and able to stick with us closer than a brother?

He said: "...if any man hear my voice." How? By reading his words? This is the beginning. We have his words, and this enables us to sit at his feet and visit with him. But reading alone is not sufficient. He said: "Ye are my friends, if ye do whatsoever I command you" (Jno. 15:14). If we fail or refuse to obey him, then we have spurned his friendship and labeled him as unwelcome.

Another way we can entertain Christ is by supplying the needs of his disciples who are "ahungered...or naked...or a stranger...or imprisoned...or sick" (Matt. 25:40).

May our visits with Christ and his friends strengthen our faith and our determination to be a better friend to One who has so clearly demonstrated that he is truly our Best Friend.

1.

"At Jesus' Feet"

VIVID details are given of three occasions when Christ visited with Mary and Martha. To them he first spoke some of the most significant eternal truths.

On one occasion he sat in their home as Martha prepared a meal. All women can visualize just how she must have felt; for the conflicts which raged within her are common to all who face the responsibilities of caring for a home. "He entered into a certain village: and a certain woman named Martha received him into her house. And she had a sister called Mary, which also sat at Jesus' feet and heard his word" (Luke 10:38,39). What a lovely scene of friendship, devotion, and hospitality.

Another picture shows us the home when death entered and took Lazarus. This is a heartache which comes in time to every home. Therefore, this account is one of the most comforting of all Scriptures. It gives a beautiful glimpse into the heart of our Lord. He wept with those he loved!

The third picture shows them at a supper just a few days before Christ's crucifixion. Surely his heart was heavy, and he sought the strength which comes from close friends in times of crisis. From this memorable evening we are given lessons of such force that their impact will be felt in eternity.

As we look at these life-like portraitures, we identify ourselves so closely with Mary and Martha — for in them we see our own responsibilities, conflicts, anxieties, sorrows, and blessings. All of us live in two realms, the material and the spiritual. In both, we have God-ordained duties. At times these areas of responsibility seem to conflict; and Christ can help us, as he did Mary and Martha, to make proper choices and to conquer daily problems. He was there as they faced life and death — cares and heartaches ranging all the way from the tension of preparing a simple meal to the intense grief which death brings.

One of the most important lessons we can learn from these two good women is to follow their example of sitting at Jesus' feet, hearing his words, and accepting his authority. This is the foundation upon which the whole of Christianity is built. Without an understanding of this one basic principle, all other lessons would be vain and superfluous.

I. THE IMPORTANCE OF AUTHORITY.

Think how essential it is to have a standard of authority in every realm. Without it, the world would be in chaos. Suppose that each person were allowed to fix his own standard of time, or to decide what constitutes an acre of land or a pound of food. Suppose there were no fixed weights and measures. Can you visualize the confusion that would result? The home where parental authority is not recognized is filled with confusion. A nation whose people disregard governmental authority is engulfed in crime. A recognition of authority is absolutely essential in every secular realm if there is to be order or peace. How much more important it is in the spiritual realm.

Using different standards of authority is the most fundamental cause of religious division today, and no question can be resolved until a basis of authority is agreed upon. This was the cause of confusion in the Corinthian church: "Every one of you saith, I am of Paul; and I of Apollos; and I of Cephas; and I of Christ" (I Cor. 1:12). If they would decide who was to be their authority, their contentions would cease;

for then they would "all speak the same thing" (I Cor. 1:10).

What is authority? It is the right to command and to enforce obedience. All authority is either primary, delegated or usurped, the latter being no real authority at all. The authority of God is primary. He has all power and all authority. Only that which has been delegated by him to others can be rightly exercised. Anyone who assumes authority which has not been given him by God is guilty of usurpation. It is absolutely essential for us to find out who has authority over us in spiritual matters, whom we must follow and obey, for the eternal destiny of our souls is at stake.

II. MUST WE HEAR THE WORDS OF CHRIST?

An inspiring picture forms in our minds as we visualize Mary and Martha sitting at Jesus' feet and listening to his words, but how important is it for us to do the same? Is it an optional matter? Our nation is filled with people who feel that they can either listen to Christ, or reject him, as they choose, and that they can still be pleasing to God.

Some years ago an American statesman was lecturing on the subject: "Moral Values Which Unite Mankind." He gave a masterful presentation on ties which bind the people of the world. When he had finished and the applause subsided, a Japanese student who had been carefully taking notes arose from his seat and asked: "But, sir, what about Jesus Christ?" You could have heard a pin drop. Everybody in the hall got the point. Here was a great statesman representing a supposedly Christian nation, but he had not said one word about the necessity of Jesus Christ in establishing the moral values that can unite mankind.

Most of the religious world today attempts to strip Christ of his deity and authority and to relegate him to the place of a mere man, a good man worthy of emulation, but just a man. Such a position is impossible, for one who rejects the deity and authority of Christ rejects the whole core of the Bible, which leaves nothing. Jesus is the central figure of the Bible. The Old Testament points forward to his coming. The New Testament points backward to his having come. If you take him and his authority out of the Bible, you have only a shell. Consider the following:

Jesus is the Prophet, raised up from among the people, mentioned in the Old Testament prophecies as the one the world would have to hear to be saved: "I will raise them up a Prophet from among their brethren, like unto thee, and will put my words in his mouth, and he shall speak unto them all that I shall command him. And it shall come to pass, that whosoever will not hearken unto my words which he shall speak in my name, I will require it of him" (Deut. 18:18,19). How do we know this refers to Christ? It is quoted in Acts 3:22-26 and definitely says it means Christ. It further says: "Every soul which will not hear that Prophet shall be destroyed from among the people" (ver. 23). This is understandable. If he is the Saviour, we must hear him to be saved; then to refuse to hear him is to be destroyed.

God has spoken to us in these last days (days of the Christian dispensation) through his Son (Heb. 1:1,2). Thus at the transfiguration God broke his silence by speaking out from on high: "This is my beloved Son in whom I am well pleased; hear ye him" (Matt. 17:5). It is evident from the context that there was a time when man was to listen to Moses and Elias; but, all of that having been fulfilled, the day was to come in which God would speak to the world through his Son. Nothing can be more authoritative than this. No wonder his mother said of him, "Whatsoever he saith unto you, do it" (Jno. 2:5).

The claims Jesus made reveal the authority he possessed. For instance:

(1) He claimed to be the Son of God — not just a mere man (Jno. 5:23). If true, he was the Son of God and a good man. If false, he was neither; for good men do not lie. Modernists who deny the Sonship of Christ on the one hand and accept his goodness on the other crucify themselves on two opposite beams of irreconcilable views.

(2) Christ made four broad and strong claims in John 14:6: "I am the way, the truth, and the life" — three claims; and, this being true, he added the fourth: "No man cometh unto the Father, but by me." So it is either sit at the feet of Christ and hear his words or be forever barred from the Father.

(3) He said that he was the door of entrance: "Verily, verily, I say unto you, He that entereth not by the door into the sheepfold, but climbeth up some other way, the same is a thief and a robber . . . I am the door; by me if any man enter in, he shall be saved" (Jno. 10:1-10).

(4) Our Lord made the claim that his words possessed the power of life: "The words that I speak unto you, they are spirit, and they are life" (Jno. 6:63). The Word is spoken of as seed (Lk. 8:11) and as such has the germinal power of life. It is not a dead message, but rather the power to provide everlasting life and Jesus said so in John 12:49,50.

(5) Jesus claimed all authority: "All power [authority, A. S. V.] is given unto me in heaven and in earth" (Matt. 28:18).

(6) In one of the most beautiful figures, Christ further testifies of his authority when he says: "I am the good shepherd: the good shepherd giveth his life for the sheep" (Jno. 10:11). The shepherd always has authority over the sheep.

The shepherd commands; the sheep obey. The shepherd leads; the sheep follow. Millions have marvelled at the simplicity and grandeur of the 23rd Psalm and from it have received comfort and consolation; but we cannot fully comprehend its impact until we come to the New Testament and become personally acquainted with the Shepherd, who "leadeth me" with such concern, tenderness and love that he was willing to lay down his life for the sheep. Look at the glorious rewards promised to those who will follow this authoritative Leader:

> He maketh me to lie down in green pastures: he leadeth me beside the still waters. He restoreth my soul: he leadeth me in the paths of righteousness for his name's sake. Yea, though I walk through the valley of the shadow of death, I will fear no evil: for thou art with me; thy rod and thy staff they comfort me.
>
> Thou preparest a table before me in the presence of mine enemies: thou anointest my head with oil; my cup runneth over. Surely goodness and mercy shall follow me all the days of my life: and I shall dwell in the house of the Lord for ever.   — Psa. 23:2-6.

Read again those comforting words and consider the rewards to be gained in this life and the ones to be enjoyed in the next world — all dependent upon the sheep's willingness to hear the commands of the Shepherd; and this Shepherd is Christ.

(7) The Saviour stated that his word would judge us: "He that rejecteth me, and receiveth not my words, hath one that judgeth him: the word that I have spoken, the same shall judge him in the last day" (Jno. 12:48). If he is the Saviour, and he is, then his words save or condemn; and we must face them at the judgment.

Today we hear strange things indeed, for many who claim to follow Christ are pushing hard for what they call the "brotherhood of man" — by this they mean an acceptance of all things in religion, such as revealed in the language of one modernist teacher: "I think the time is not too far distant when we who are Christians will recognize Buddhism, Mohammedanism, Judaism and all other religions as other roads to God." This is impossible! If Christ is anything, he is everything. If he did not speak the truth, we should reject him completely. If he did speak the truth, this excludes modernism's way of accepting God and rejecting Christ — appreciating him and depreciating him at the same time. It excludes all other "roads to God."

III. CHRIST DELEGATED AUTHORITY TO THE APOSTLES.

Christ received all authority from the Father, but we must go further to understand all God's teaching on the subject of authority. Are we obligated to obey the words of Peter, Paul, James and John? Did they speak of themselves, or did they speak the words of God? Some people have the mistaken idea that they need to obey only the red-letter words in their Bible (the words of Christ).

A lady who writes a regular newspaper column on religion was quoting a passage from Corinthians, written by Paul, and she made a statement something like this: "So spoke Paul, and some would have us to believe that so spoke God."

The Bible teaches that a rejection of the apostles is actually a rejection of God. Christ said to them: "He that receiveth you receiveth me; and he that receiveth me receiveth him that sent me" (Matt. 10:40). "He that heareth you heareth me; and he that despiseth you despiseth me; and he that despiseth me despiseth him that sent me" (Lk. 10:16). This was spoken to the twelve apostles, but Paul was also an apostle (Rom. 1:1; 11:13; I Cor. 9:1).

Christ gave his word to the apostles. "For I have given

unto them the words thou gavest me; and they have received them, and have known surely that I came out from thee . . . I have given them thy word" (Jno. 17:8,14).

Notice Christ's promise to the apostles:"I have yet many things to say unto you, but ye cannot bear them now. Howbeit when he, the Spirit of truth is come, he will guide you into all truth: for he shall not speak of himself; but whatsoever he shall hear, that shall he speak: and he will show you things to come" (Jno. 16:12-15).

Christ did not reveal all things while he was here in the flesh, but rather promised that he would send the Holy Spirit upon the apostles to guide them into "all truth," after he went back to heaven. The record of this fulfilled promise is found in Acts 2, and the words they spoke were authoritative. They did not speak their own words or thoughts, but "as the Spirit gave them utterance" (Acts 2:4).

On another occasion Christ said to the apostles: "Whatsoever ye shall bind on earth shall be bound in heaven; and whatsoever ye shall loose on earth shall be loosed in heaven" (Matt. 18:18). This was given to all the apostles, though the same promise had previously been given to Peter (Matt. 16:19). Peter was promised nothing which was not also promised to all the apostles. Does this promise mean that the apostles could decide for themselves what they wanted to bind and loose? No. It was bound by virtue of the fact that they were guided by the Holy Spirit. The binding and loosing was the work of the Holy Spirit as such worked through them, in keeping with Christ's promise in John 14:26; 15:26; 16:13; and Luke 24:46-49.

IV. CONCLUSION.

We should sit with Mary and Martha at the feet of Jesus, understanding the essentiality and finality of truth as he spoke it and later revealed it through the apostles.

No lesson is more fundamental, for upon it is built the whole superstructure of Christianity.

REVIEW EXERCISE

1. What caused confusion in the Corinthian church?...... ....

....

2. Give the definition of authority. ....

....

3. To whom belongs primary authority? ....

4. One who assumes authority not given to him is guilty of................

5. "This is my beloved..............., in whom I am well pleased; ....

...." Who said this? ....

6. "Whosoever will not hearken unto .... words which...............

shall speak in my name, I will require it of him." Who is the

one which must be heard?......... .... Scripture: ....

7. "No man cometh unto the Father, but by ...." Scripture:

....

8. (T or F) The sheep have the authority to tell the shepherd what they want to do.

9. What did Jesus' mother say concerning his authority?.... ....

....

10. (T or F) Christ excludes all other roads to God.

11. Christ promised the apostles he would send the Holy Spirit who would guide them into "................... truth."

12. Who were promised the power to "bind and loose"?...................

....

13. Explain why it is impossible and inconsistent to take the posi-

tion that Christ was a good man but not the Son of God. ....

--- ....

--- ------------ --------- ....

FOR THOUGHT OR DISCUSSION

1. Read I John 1:1-3 and discuss John's testimony concerning Christ. They had seen, had heard, and had handled evidence from which they concluded that Christ was truly the Son of God.

2. What are some ways people usurp authority which God has not given to them? In the home? In the church? To understand the seriousness of this, study the sin of Aaron and Miriam (Num. 12:1-15).

3. The name Martha does not appear in the Old Testament. Neither does the name Mary, but some have thought it to be a derivative of the older name of Miriam. Since there are so many in the New Testament named Mary, much discussion has arisen. Some have tried to identify the sister of Lazarus as the sinful woman in Luke 7:36-50. There is nothing to support this. Also, we quote the following from Smith's Bible Dictionary: "Mary Magdalene has become the type of a class of repentant sinners; but there is no authority for identifying her with the 'sinner' who anointed the feet of Jesus in Luke 7:36-50; neither is there any authority for the supposition that Mary Magdalene is the same as the sister of Lazarus. Neither of these theories has the slightest foundation in fact."

2.

"And Heard His Word"

MARY and Martha sat at Jesus' feet and heard his word. We are not told all Jesus said to them that day, but we know that whatever he said was in harmony with all his recorded teachings. It may be that he said some of the same things he taught on other occasions. May we listen to his words, just as Mary and Martha did. In this study we can discuss only a few.

I. "BE YE ALSO READY."

On one occasion Christ admonished: "Therefore be ye also ready: for in such an hour as ye think not the Son of man cometh" (Matt. 24:44).

Ready for what? Ready for the second coming of Christ, which will bring the end to this world and the final judgment day. Ready to give an account of the deeds done in the body (Rom. 14:12). This testifies of consummation, accountability and immortality — that we need to be ready for something else.

Our stay here is brief. "For what is your life? It is even a vapor, that appeareth for a little time, and then vanisheth away" (Jas. 4:14). "Man that is born of woman is of few days, and full of trouble. He cometh forth like a flower, and is cut down: he fleeth also as a shadow, and continueth not" (Job 14:1,2). "The days of our years are threescore years and ten; and if by reason of strength they be fourscore years, yet is their strength labor and sorrow; for it is soon cut off and we fly away" (Psa. 90:10). It doesn't pay to fall too much in love with this world, because we shall soon have to leave it. Even the atheist knows that he will not be here long.

Man's innate sense of incompleteness testifies of immortality. No matter what man may enjoy or attain, he still has a feeling of unfulfilled longings. An animal may graze until full and lie down in the shade in perfect contentment; but a human being may accumulate wealth, power and prestige, satisfy every fleshly appetite and lie down in the shade to rest — and there is still a feeling of unrest and incompleteness, a reach for something that lies beyond the grasp of this world. This is because man is immortal and the animal is not. Solomon keenly felt this emptiness of life, in spite of all he did to try to fill it. This is because this world is not our real home. We are but pilgrims and strangers here (Heb. 11:13; I Pet. 2:11) — and pilgrims and strangers are not at home. No wonder Christ admonishes: "Be ye ready:" It's the only wise thing to do (Matt. 7:24-27).

A little girl came home one day and was told that her father had gone to heaven. She replied: "I don't understand. Daddy always talked about the trips he was going to take, but I never heard him mention anything about taking a trip to heaven."

The peoples of all nations possess the fond hope of immortality. An innate longing for the continuity of life in more pleasant circumstances refuses to be quieted by a fast moving span of days lived in sin and sorrow, struggle and strife — and some joys, enough to make them dream and hope for a world where no sorrow will ever enter. This was true of the American Indian; he hoped for the Happy Hunting Ground. This instinctive feeling can be explained only in the light of man's nature. He is not an animal. He was created in the image of God. He possesses a spirit this world can never satisfy (Eccl. 12:5,7).

III. CHRIST'S THREE GREAT INVITATIONS.

Christ has given to us, as immortal beings journeying to eternity, all the instructions we need. His teachings may be summed up in his three great invitations: (1) "Come unto me," (2) "Come after me," and finally (3) "Come, ye blessed of my Father, inherit the kingdom prepared for you from the foundation of the world." The last invitation will be extended only to those who have accepted the first two.

"Come unto me." This is the greatest invitation of the ages. You may have received invitations which thrilled and delighted you, but nothing can begin to compare with the significance and grandeur of this one. To whom was it given? "All ye that labor and are heavy laden" (Matt. 11:28). Surely this includes us and all mankind. So many things trouble and envelop the heart with unrest, as discussed in Chapters IX and X, and our burdened spirits cry out for relief. What are we to do? "Take my yoke upon you." How can one find rest by assuming a yoke? He trades the yoke of sin for the yoke of Christ.

Why should man bear any yoke? Why not throw off all shackles and declare oneself in bondage to nothing? Multitudes are attempting to do this — even some modern theologians are declaring that man should be subject to no restrictions, feel no inhibitions, be completely free. What they fail to understand is that everybody is a slave, a servant. If one claims all freedom and submits to no restrictions, then he is a slave of his own passions and ambitions, and the yoke he bears is indeed heavy. This is amply borne out in testimony of many who have tried it, only to come to the end of life disillusioned, embittered and fearful. Many have despaired of life and died at their own hands. They declared themselves free but actually became so shackled by their own chains that they sank in the mire of sin and hopelessness.

All who are not servants of righteousness are servants of sin (Rom. 6:16-18). The person who thinks he serves no one is only fooling himself. He is serving sin and Satan, and the only wages Satan can pay is death: "The wages of sin is death" (Rom. 6:23).

Christ is quite frank to declare that he offers a yoke and a burden, but he also promises that it is lighter and more bearable than the yoke of sin.

> Make me a captive, Lord
> And then I shall be free;
> Force me to render up my sword,
> And I shall conqueror be.
> I sink in life's alarms
> When by myself I stand;
> Imprison me within thine arms,
> And strong shall be my hand.
> — George Matheson

How does one throw off his yoke of sin and come to Christ? Christ said: "He that believeth and is baptized shall be saved" (Mk. 16:16). This is the way the great apostle Paul was freed of his sin (Acts 22:16), for man contacts the saving blood of Christ by being baptized into Christ's death (Rom. 6:3,4), the place where the blood was shed.

"Come after me." It is not sufficient merely to accept Christ's first invitation. We must also follow him. "And he said unto all, If any man would come after me, let him deny himself, and take up his cross daily and follow me" (Lk. 9:23). This necessitates concerted and scripturally directed effort.

(1) Being a real Christian requires more strength, conviction, courage and perseverance than anything else in the world. It cannot be done by weaklings; but its attainment brings true happiness and abundant living.

True happiness (if understood)
Consists alone in doing good.

It took great courage for godly men of old to stand in the face of hardships. Think of such men as Noah, Joseph, Daniel and Paul. They possessed great conviction, strength and courage. A Bible teacher asked her students why the lions did not eat Daniel. One little boy answered: "It was because most of him was backbone, and the rest of him was grit."

Great strength and courage are required to follow such words of Christ as these:

"Love your enemies, bless them that curse you, do good to them that hate you, and pray for them which despitefully use you, and persecute you" (Matt. 5:44).

"But I say unto you, That ye resist not evil: but whosoever shall smite thee on thy right cheek, turn to him the other also" (Matt. 5:39). Our first impulse always is to "get even" when one has wronged us, and it takes much faith and courage to let the Lord take care of all retribution. Yet, this is commanded: "Recompense to no man evil for evil" (Rom. 12:17). "Avenge not yourselves, but rather give place unto wrath: for it is written, Vengeance is mine; I will repay, saith the Lord" (Rom. 12:19).

"Therefore if thou bring thy gift to the altar, and there rememberest that thy brother hath aught against thee; leave there thy gift before the altar and go thy way; first be reconciled to thy brother, and then come and offer thy gift" (Matt. 5:23,24). This, too, takes courage. It teaches that when one has wronged his fellowman, his worship is not acceptable until he has righted that wrong. What does it mean for a brother to have "aught against thee"? Does this apply simply because one may not like us or may violently disagree with us, or because we may have enemies?? Not necessarily. Christ

had enemies. Did he have to be reconciled to them before he
could worship? No. Why? Because his enemies did not
actually have "aught against" Christ. He had not sinned
against them in any way, but they became his enemies because
of the sin in their own hearts. Therefore, this Scripture applies when a wrong has been committed against a fellowman,
not merely to an imaginary grievance which may exist in the
mind of the aggrieved one.

(2) "Let him deny himself, and take up his cross daily and
follow me." Self-denial is one of the most difficult of all commands, for all of us have a natural tendency to pamper self
rather than deny self. Usually we fail to understand that self-
denial is in our own good interest, for it promotes spiritual
growth.

John Morley, English statesman, said: "The great business
of life is to be, to do, and to do without." A tourist traveled
to a remote village and went to the local inn for the night.
He was given a kerosene lamp and shown to a bed amid bare
surroundings. The innkeeper's final instructions were: "If
there is anything you need, let us know; and we will show you
how to do without it."

> Man needs but little here below
> Nor needs that little long.

However, self-denial involves much more than material
things. In fact, this is probably the easiest aspect of self-denial.
The appetites and inclinations of the flesh must oftentimes be
denied. Men marveled at Christ's ability to deny self, to
refuse the temptation to turn stones into bread at a time of
intense hunger. There are times when we must deny self of
sleep, social activities, popularity or the approval of fellowman
in order to put the Lord first. At other times we must deny
self the luxury of speech, when we are tempted to speak that
which should never pass the lips.

"Come, ye blessed of my Father, inherit the kingdom prepared for you from the foundation of the world" (Matt. 25:34). This is a picture of the final judgment day, and this glorious invitation will be extended only to those who have accepted the first two invitations: "Come unto me," and "Come after me."

III. CHRIST'S WORDS OF WARNING.

If we sit at Jesus' feet and hear his words, we should heed his words of warning. We mention only two.

"Except ye repent, ye shall all likewise perish" (Lk. 13:3). Repentance is probably the hardest spiritual command to obey. Even though one may be convinced of error or misdeeds, it is very difficult to bring the heart to genuine repentance. Yet this is necessary in becoming a Christian, and likewise a prerequisite of forgiveness for a Christian. Therefore, every sin of which man has not repented will face him in the judgment.

What is repentance? It is a change of heart produced by godly sorrow for sins and followed by a reformation of life. It is not sufficient just to be sorry that something has been done. We must be sorry that we have violated the law of God, turn from the sin, and then change our lives to reflect that resolution. This requires much humility. One too proud to admit a mistake or sin must forever remain outside God's realm of forgiveness. We must bring our hearts to genuine submission and willingness to say: "God, be merciful to me, a sinner," striving then to put away whatever specific sin we have discovered in our lives.

"Enter ye in at the strait gate: for wide is the gate, and broad is the way, that leadeth to destruction, and many there be which go in thereat: because strait is the gate, and narrow is the way, which leadeth unto life, and few there be that find

it" (Matt. 7:13,14). These are fearful words. We are in-
clined to feel that most people are pretty good and therefore
headed for heaven. Jesus warned that most people will go
to the judgment unprepared and therefore lost, while only a
few will be prepared. This is a warning to be diligent in our
efforts to be among the few.

IV. CHRIST'S WORDS OF COMFORT.

While we hear Christ's commands and heed his warnings,
how glorious it is to hear also his words of comfort. Without
them, we would not have courage to go on. Think on the
comforting and peace-bestowing power of Christ's promises
to the faithful:

"In the world ye shall have tribulation; but be of good
cheer; I have overcome the world" (Jno. 16:33).

"Peace I leave with you, my peace I give unto you: not
as the world giveth, give I unto you. Let not your heart be
troubled, neither let it be afraid" (Jno. 14:27).

"And Jesus answered and said, Verily I say unto you,
There is no man that hath left houses, or brethren, or sisters,
or father, or mother, or wife, or children, or lands, for my
sake, and the gospel's, but he shall receive an hundredfold
now in this time, houses and brethren, and sisters, and mothers,
and children, and lands, with persecutions; and in the world
to come eternal life" (Mk. 19:29,30).

"Ye shall be sorrowful, but your sorrow shall be turned
into joy" (Jno. 16:20).

"Let not your heart be troubled: ye believe in God, believe also in me. In my Father's house are many mansions:
if it were not so, I would have told you. I go to prepare a
place for you. And if I go and prepare a place for you, I will
come again, and receive you unto myself; that where I am,
there ye may be also" (Jno. 14:1-3).

6. "Lo, I am with you alway, even unto the end of the world" (Matt. 28:20).

REVIEW EXERCISE

1. For what are we admonished to be ready? _____

2. "The wages of sin is _____."

3. Everyone is either a servant of _____ or a servant of_____

4. Give Christ's three great invitations: _____

_____

_____

5. What was Paul told to do to have his sins washed away?_____

_____ Scripture: _____

7. (T or ..F) There is nothing which can keep man's worship from being acceptable to God.

8. What is repentance? _____

_____

9. "Do good to them that _____ you.'

10. All who do not repent will _____.

11. To what does James compare our life? _____

12. To what does Job compare our life? _____

13. How many people will be saved? _____

14. We are but _____ and _____ in this world.

FOR THOUGHT OR DISCUSSION

1. In your opinion, what are some of the most difficult commands of God to obey?

2. Think of words of warning given by Christ, in addition to those mentioned in the lesson.

3. When you become blue and discouraged, go to town and go through

a large department store. Don't count the things you would like to have. Rather, make mental note of all the things you can do without. You will go home more grateful for all the things you have.

3.

Following His Steps

CHRIST "suffered for us, leaving us an example, that ye should follow his steps" (I Pet. 2:21). This is one reason he came into the world. So many times he not only invited but commanded man to follow him (Matt. 4:19; 8:22; 9:9; Mk. 10:21; Jno. 1:43; 21:22; 12:26).

It was not sufficient for Mary and Martha merely to sit at Jesus' feet and hear his words. They had to arise and follow his steps. So do we. To fail is folly: "Every one that heareth these sayings of mine, and doeth them not, shall be likened to a foolish man which built his house upon the sand" (Matt. 7:26).

Men have pursued the art of living, but none mastered it completely except our Lord. It is amazing and inspiring to study his life, to watch as he handled the problems of living and emerged always the victor. He walked serenely through this trouble-filled world and into the portals of glory. We should gladly and wholeheartedly follow his steps.

I. BECAUSE CHRIST IS OUR EXAMPLE AND GUIDE.

Mankind has always felt a need for someone to show the way to live. Christ did this. He does not ask us to go anywhere he did not go, bear any burden he has not borne or demand any sacrifice he has not made.

> If washed in Jesus' blood,
> Then bear his likeness too,
> And as you onward press
> Ask, What would Jesus do?
> Be brave to do the right,
> And scorn to be untrue;
> When fear would whisper, Yield
> Ask, What would Jesus do?

Christ has furnished an inspiring example:

In ministering to others. "Even as the Son of man came not to be ministered unto, but to minister, and to give his life a ransom for many" (Matt. 20:28).

In humility. "If I then, your Lord and Master, have washed your feet; ye also ought to wash one another's feet. For I have given you an example, that ye should do as I have done to you" (Jno. 13:14,15).

In love for fellowman. "A new commandment I give unto you, That ye love one another; as I have loved you, that ye also love one another" (Jno. 13:34).

In soul-saving and missionary zeal. "As thou has sent me into the world, even so have I also sent them into the world" (Jno. 17:18).

In unselfish consideration of others. "Let every one of us please his neighbor for his good to edification. For even Christ pleased not himself" (Rom. 15:2,3).

In obedience to God. "Let this mind be in you, which was also in Christ . . . humbled himself, and became obedient unto death, even the death of the cross" (Phil. 2:5-8).

In forgiveness. "Forbearing one another, and forgiving one another, if any man have a quarrel against any: even as Christ forgave you, so also do ye" (Col. 3:13).

In bearing persecution. "For consider him that endured such contradiction of sinners against himself, lest ye be wearied and faint in your minds" (Heb. 12:3). "Who when he was reviled, reviled not again" (I Pet. 2:23).

In purity and holiness. "As he which hath called you is holy, so be ye holy in all manner of conversation" (I Pet. 1:15). "Every man that hath this hope in him purifieth himself, even as he is pure" (I Jno. 3:3).

In complete victory. "To him that overcometh will I grant to sit with me in my throne, even as I also overcame, and am set down with my Father in his throne" (Rev. 3:21).

II. BECAUSE CHRIST IS OUR SAVIOR.

This One who asks us to follow him loved us enough to die for us (Rom. 5:8,9). Without his willingness to die, we would be hopelessly lost in sin. The world has almost lost sight of the problem of sin. We are being told on every hand that there is no fixed standard of right and wrong, that nothing is sinful within itself. But what is sin? It is rebellion against God. It may be either a violation of God's law (I Jno. 3:4) or an omission of his commandments (Jas. 4:17). Everybody is guilty of these transgressions (Rom. 3:23). For this reason, everyone is lost apart from the blood of Christ (Eph. 1:7).

How we should love and appreciate and gladly follow our Savior.

III. BECAUSE JESUS IS OUR SYMPATHETIC FRIEND.

Our hearts long for friendship. We need the feeling that others are interested and concerned about our welfare. Some of the sweetest relationships of life are enjoyed by friends whose hearts are united in purpose, in Christian fellowship and in love. If we are following Christ, he is our constant friend "who sticketh closer than a brother." To sympathize means "to feel with." Christ sympathizes with all our heart's longings, for he has felt them too.

Sympathetic in sorrow. When grief envelops our hearts, does Jesus care? He cared so much that he wept with Mary and Martha at the death of Lazarus (Jno. 11:35). He wept not because he could not raise Lazarus, for he did. He wept because he had a great sympathetic heart in tune with the sufferings of mankind that on this occasion vibrated with the grief of Mary and Martha. This spirit that Jesus exemplified is essential to Christian living (Rom. 12:15).

Sympathetic in temptation. He was "tempted in all points like as we are" (Heb. 4:15). No temptation can beset us which he has not already met and conquered. No matter what our sin or temptation is, Jesus can understand its pull on the human heart.

Sympathetic in physical weariness. He became tired, hungry and thirsty, just as we do. He fasted forty days (Matt. 4:1,2). He prayed all night. He slept in the midst of a storm. He understands the intense fatigue which can envelop the body and spirit of us all.

Sympathetic in loneliness. He went through Gethsemane alone, but the pinnacle of loneliness was reached on the cross when even the Father turned away from the Son as the sins of the world were laid upon him; and we hear the loneliest cry to pass anyone's lips: "My God, my God, why hast thou forsaken me?" (Matt. 27:46).

Sympathetic in disappointment. As Christ was in Gethsemane, he longed for friends to care, to understand and to stand by him in his darkest hours. When he emerged and found his dearest friends asleep, he said: "Could ye not watch with me one hour?" (Matt. 26:40). Judas, another close friend, betrayed him into the enemies' hand.

Sympathetic in death. Christ felt the natural shrinking from the ordeal of death: "If it be possible, let this cup pass from me" (Matt. 26:39). When our dearest friends and loved ones have gone with us as far as they can, to the very brink of the grave, then our sympathetic Friend can take our hand and lead us through the valley of the shadow of death (Matt. 28:20).

IV. BECAUSE CHRIST IS OUR MEDIATOR.

This Friend of all friends intercedes before the Father in behalf of his followers (Heb. 4:15,16).

We do not know the author of the following article, but we feel sure that he would want to share it with you.

THE DAY I WAS ARRESTED

When I was a little boy of two, my mother died. When I was four, my father died. I was living here and there. I was almost fourteen years of age, and it was Christmas week when I was caught in sin and put under arrest and dragged to court.

I did not cry. I had cried all the tears out of my head. I tried to look at the judge. I wished I could faint. I was guilty. I did not have a friend. I was miserable. They packed the courthouse. They looked at me, then at the judge. Their faces seemed to say: "Judge, give him the full penalty of the law and save trouble later on." I felt as though the whole universe was down on me.

By and by a clerk stood up and said, "This court is open." The judge said, "Has this boy anyone to represent him?" I did not know the meaning of this. They said, "No." I was hopeful. The judge said to a lawyer, "I appoint you to take this boy's case." The lawyer walked through the crowd, pushed the policeman aside and took me into a room. I sank into a corner. I thought he was going to drag me to execution. But I saw tears under his eyelashes. He sat down and slipped his arm around me. It was the tenderest touch I ever felt, and it drew me to him.

"My little friend, are you guilty?" he asked.

I could not have lied to him to save the world. He gave me a little squeeze. I said, "Yes, sir, I am guilty and lots more they don't know about." When I looked at him, I could not lie. I had found a friend. I can feel his hand yet. Oh! it was such a wonderful touch to an orphan child.

He said, "Don't you think you had better confess guilty and throw yourself on the mercy of the court?"

I did not know what that meant, but I thought if he would throw me, it was best. I said, "Please, sir, throw me on the mercy of the court."

He put his hand on my head, and I put out my dirty claw-like fingers and grabbed his coat, and the feeling came to me that if I could hang on to his coat he would pull me through.

He came to the judge and said, "If it please your Honor, it has been my privilege to practice before this bar for many years. I have noticed that when the ends of justice can be secured, it is your Honor's custom to show mercy. I stand with this trembling orphan child, without father or mother, home or friend, to beg your Honor's mercy. His heart is broken. He confesses with readiness his sin. He pleads for forgiveness."

I grabbed some more coat. I thought it was a great speech. It was just an introductory remark. He spoke until silence fell everywhere. He spoke until the most beautiful language filled every corner of the court. He spoke until old men wept. He spoke until my policeman was brushing tears from his cheeks. He spoke until he said, "If you will show compassion on this orphan child, I pledge your Honor, to look after his education and his upbringing and give to society a useful citizen." He spoke until my heart burst within me for love and admiration for my friend. I thought if I could put my ragged coatsleeves around his neck and kiss his cheek one time, they could take me and hang me and I would die happy.

Then came the greatest shock of all. The lawyer spoke again to the judge and said, "My father." That shot through me like a bolt of lightning! The judge had appointed his own son to plead for me.

"My father," he continued, "The intenseness of my love
for my little client comes from the fact that he is my brother."
I wasn't much on mathematics, but I could see at once that
if the judge on the bench was the father of the attorney,
and the attorney was my brother, then the judge was my
father too! I gave a shout. I made a leap. Then the judge
stood up and said, "Rejoice, for the lost is found, and the
dead is alive."

This scene rends our hearts. As you come to the close of it,
you understand that it did not literally happen; but you also
recognize that in principle it is true and applies to each of us.
We are the orphan sinners. Without the mercy of our
Father, and without the help of our Mediator who is also our
Brother, we would be hopelessly lost in sin. How gratefully
we should follow his steps.

IV. BECAUSE CHRIST WILL BE OUR JUDGE.

Another important reason we should gladly follow Jesus
is that some day we shall stand before him in judgment (Matt.
25:31,32). This is inescapable. It includes you and me.

When that time comes, it will be wonderful to know that
the Judge is on our side and that we are on his side.

V. WHERE DO JESUS' STEPS LEAD US?

They lead us through the waters of baptism. Many today
who claim to follow Jesus' steps mock and ridicule the idea of
baptism. This is inconsistent, for Christ saw the necessity
of baptism. Though he had no sins, he could not "fulfill all
righteousness" without baptism (Matt. 3:13-15). Neither
can we; and if we follow Jesus' steps, they will lead us through
the waters of baptism. He not only practiced it, he commanded it (Mk. 16:16).

Jesus' steps lead us to worship. Even as a lad he went
into the synagogue. Later he went to the place of worship
and stood up to read the law (Lk. 4:16). No person can

follow his steps and at the same time absent himself from public worship. If the Son of God felt a need for regular communion with the Father, how much more should we in our weakness and frailty yearn for the same strength and sustenance. Surely the Father understood this need and for this reason commanded: "Not forsaking the assembling of ourselves together" (Heb. 10:25).

Christ's steps lead to the sin-laden and downcast. We see him at Jacob's well where he offered to a sinful woman the water of life which could satisfy her starving soul (Jno. 4:5-26). He did not have a "holier than thou" attitude, but rather his heart reached out in love and sympathy toward those bogged down in the sinfulness of sin. He was not afraid to be seen extending to them a helping hand, though he was criticized for it (Matt. 9:11,12).

Christ's steps lead through Gethsemane. There will be times of intense trial and heartache. The way to heaven has its Gethsemanes and we shall be wounded along the way; but he who was wounded, too, has a balm for our every hurt.

If Jesus' steps had ended at the cross, think of the dark hopelessness that would have engulfed humanity. Thank God that such is not true. Our hearts leap with joy as we read of his triumph over death and the grave, and we watch as *his steps lead into the portals of heaven* (Acts 1:9,10). This is the greatest motivating power for our following him down the stony and stormy path of life. We can see the end of the road! It was to Martha that Christ gave his reassuring promises concerning the resurrection: "I am the resurrection, and the life: he that believeth in me, though he were dead, yet shall he live" (Jno. 11:25).

Christ is the only way to triumph over life, death and the grave. He is the only way to heaven. If we follow Satan, we shall be led into sins and more sins, defeats and more defeats, and finally into torment (Rev. 20:10). If we follow philosophers, we can be lifted no higher than humans can reach. But if we follow Christ, we follow the only one who has been to the other side of the river of death and returned to tell us the way. So confidently we press onward with the assurance of the apostle Paul who said: "I know whom I have believed, and am persuaded that he is able to keep that which I have committed unto him against that day" (II Tim. 1:12).

REVIEW EXERCISE

1. How did Christ demonstrate a spirit of humble service?................

----

2. (T or F) Christ did whatever pleased him.

3. How should we forgive one another? ....

4. How did Christ manifest his complete obedience to the Father?

----

5. When Christ was reviled, he ....

6. How did Christ show his sympathy for Mary and Martha? ....

----

7. What is the loneliest sentence in the Bible? ....

----

8. (T or F) Christ cannot understand our temptations.

9. Who is the mediator between us and God? ....

    Scripture: ....

10. (T or F) Christ did not think baptism was important.

11. What does Hebrews 10:25 teach concerning the worship? ....

----

12. How does Christ refer to himself in John 11:25? ....

13. Who "purifieth himself"? ....

14. Where do Satan's steps lead? ....

15. Name some of the ways Christ furnished the perfect example
for us to follow. ....

....

....

FOR THOUGHT OR DISCUSSION

1. Suppose a college student faces an important examination, one
upon which hangs his whole career. Suppose the professor
should hand him a book and say, "You will be judged by the
things written in this book." How diligently do you think the
student would study the book? By what Book will we some day
be judged?

2. Some today think of sin as that which is either ill-mannered
or illegal. What is sin as defined by God? Is it possible for
something to be legal; that is, permitted by the laws of the
land, and still be sinful in God's sight?

4.

All Things to Enjoy

EACH of us sustains an inescapable and necessary relationship to material things. We live in a material world and daily deal with material values. From early childhood we use money and all things it can buy. Therefore, no topic is closer to our everyday lives than the problem of learning what God has to say on this topic.

There are two extreme views. Some enthrone material possessions in their hearts until they become the god of their lives. On the other hand, some have gone to the other extreme and have labeled all material prosperity and possessions as evil and Satanic. Both views are contrary to God's word.

I. GOD IS THE CREATOR AND PROVIDER OF ALL MATERIAL BLESSINGS.

When the Lord made Adam, he placed him in a material world and showered him with every blessing. Our bodies are material and therefore require material sustenance. Adam needed food, clothing and shelter. These are not evil, but good, and were provided by a loving Father "who giveth us richly all things to enjoy" (I Tim. 6:17). Adam's enjoyment of these blessings was not sinful but was a part of his compliance with the law of God.

"God that made the world and all things therein" (Acts 17:24). Every material thing in the world was put here by God. Man can only change its form and determine its use. He can create nothing. Just one look at the world convinces us that God wants us to enjoy that which he created for us. As you drive across the plains of West Texas on land as level as a table and see the grain that reaches out for miles and waves in the breeze, you have a symbolic waving of the hand of God and an invitation to behold and take and enjoy. As you drive through the great oil fields of East Texas and see energy flowing from the ground, once again you praise the name of God who has furnished man all his needs. As you visit the great ranches of our nation and see the cattle on many hills, once again you have living evidence of God's concern for man. You visit a steel mill and think of all the blessings it brings mankind and you realize that it is God who provided the ore which makes possible the mighty structures. As you walk into a supermarket and see a thousand kinds of food, again you see evidence of the goodness of God, and it deepens our appreciation of what he has done for man.

It is thrilling and interesting to remember that God is also the creator of the beautiful things in the world. Think of some of them. Have you ever wondered why God created color? He could have made the whole world in drab black or brown or gray, but he has filled it with vibrant colors which adorn our surroundings and lift our spirits. Have you wondered why He made flowers? Many kinds of flowers fill the universe with color and fragrance, plants which evidently were not created for utilitarian purposes but simply for the enjoyment of mankind and to help fill the esthetic needs placed within man by this same Creator.

The beauty and symmetry of form came from an All-wise Maker. Have you ever marveled at the graceful form and movement of the tiger, lion, horse and many other animals? Have you ever looked at the beautiful face and figure of a little child and felt the awe of One who designed the human body? Have you ever contemplated the origin of the beauty of sound? The most lovely music in the world is the human voice. Musical instruments were invented as copies and imitations of these sounds created by God. You may think of the most impressive works of art ever created by man, and all of them are but efforts to copy some phase of beauty originally made by God.

Yes, our Creator made material things, beautiful things, and therefore our enjoyment of them is not evil, but good, when kept within the proper perspective.

Let's notice some Biblical examples which show that God wants us to have the good things of life.

One of the good things of life is a home. Jesus dined in the home of Mary and Martha. Somebody had to build it. It was not evil, but good, for them to possess it, use it, and enjoy it. Simon Peter lodged in the home of Simon the tanner.

Pure underground water is one of the good things of life, and we read of Jacob's well and the blessing it was for Jesus and others. Somebody had to dig it, but the water was placed there for man's use and enjoyment.

The marine life of the oceans and seas was created for man's use. Peter and John were fishermen.

God made the herbs from which we produce various medicines. Luke was a physician and more than likely took advantage of these God-given remedies.

The grain of the field supports both animal and human life. God used Joseph as food administrator in Egypt to preserve grain for the benefit of the people.

Jesus fed the multitudes.

The early church distributed material things to those in need.

A tent is made for man, and we read that Paul worked as a tentmaker. Christ grew up in the home of a carpenter and evidently helped with that work which blesses mankind in so many ways.

A meetinghouse in which to worship God is a material thing, but a good thing. Paul met in the third story of a building for the purpose of worship.

It is good to have transportation, to be able to go from one part of the country to another. Jesus sent for a beast of burden on which he made the triumphal entry into Jerusalem.

What about the luxuries of life? Does God look upon all the luxuries as evil, and decree that godly people must live upon the bare necessities alone? When the wise men heard of the birth of Jesus, they brought to him gifts of gold, frankencense and myrrh. Their possession of these fineries is in no way condemned, though indeed it was good that they were willing to give them to the Lord. As discussed elsewhere, some of the most godly men spoken of in the Bible were men of great wealth: Abraham, Joseph, Job, and others. God has never objected to man's possessing wealth, but he has objected to wealth's possessing man.

II. SCRIPTURES WHICH PROMISE MATERIAL BLESSINGS.

God has always intended for man to enjoy the fruit of his labors. Notice some of the promises of prosperity which were given.

"Honor the Lord with thy substance and with the first-fruits of all thine increase; so shall thy barns be filled with plenty and thy presses shall burst out with new wine" (Prov. 3:9,10).

"Be thou diligent to know the state of thy flocks, and look well to thy herds . . . The lambs are for thy clothing and the goats are the price of the field. And thou shalt have goats' milk enough for thy food" (Prov. 27:23-37).

"Bring ye all the tithes into the storehouse, that there may be meat in mine house, and prove me now herewith, saith the Lord of hosts, if I will not open you the windows of heaven, and pour you out a blessing, that there shall not be room enough to receive it" (Mal. 3:10).

"For the Scripture saith, Thou shalt not muzzle the ox that treadeth out the corn. And, The laborer is worthy of his reward" (I Tim. 5:18). Even the animals were to be compensated for their labors. How much more has God intended for man to receive the reward of his work.

"Wealth gotten by vanity shall be diminished: but he that gathereth by labor shall increase" (Prov. 13:11).

"Seek ye first the kingdom of God and his righteousness; and all these things shall be added unto you" (Matt. 6:33).

III. IS IT RIGHT TO PRAY FOR SUCCESS?

We should be able to ask the Lord's blessings upon everything we do. If it is a good and right endeavor, we should invoke the aid of God in its success. Anything which cannot be prayed about should not be done. If it is right to work and make a living, it is right to ask for God's assistance in bringing about success. "Give us this day our daily bread" (Matt. 6:11).

We have examples of this. "And let the beauty of the Lord our God be upon us: and establish thou the work of our hands upon us; yea, the work of our hands establish thou it" prayed the Psalmist (Psa. 90:17). This is talking about physical work — "the work of our hands" — and the Psalmist asked the Lord to establish it, or make it successful and fruitful.

Also, "Jabez called on the God of Israel, saying, Oh that thou wouldst bless me indeed, and enlarge my coast, and that thine hand might be with me, and that thou wouldest keep me from evil, that it may not grieve me! And God granted him that which he requested" (I Chron. 4:10). Here was a man who prayed for both material and spiritual prosperity, and the Lord answered his prayer.

Surely we understand that every prayer should be permeated with the attitude: *"Thy will be done."* We should pray also for the Lord to withhold such blessings if he, in his infinite wisdom, can foresee that such would lead us away from him.

IV. BIBLICAL EXAMPLES OF RICHES AND RIGHTEOUSNESS.

The Bible tells of some men and women who were abundantly blessed by God because they put him first in their lives.

When *Solomon* was a young man about to begin his reign over God's people, the Lord asked him the one request of his heart. The young man asked for wisdom so that he could be a just and good king. Because this was uppermost in his mind, the Lord showered him also with material prosperity such as the world has seldom seen.

Job surely put God first in his life, for God himself described him as the most righteous man upon the earth at that time (Job 1:8); yet he was wealthy. After he had stood the test of faith in both prosperity and adversity, the Lord again rewarded him materially with twice the amount he previously had.

Joseph has been called the most Christ-like character of the Old Testament. Though we know he was not sinless, no specific sin is recorded against him. He was persecuted and mistreated many times. Yet his faith stood firm, and the uppermost desire in his mind was to follow divine com-

mandments. He was godly and wealthy — one can be both.
God showered him not only with material abundance but
also with a place of prominence among his fellowmen.

The worthy woman described in Proverbs 31 was both
righteous and rich. She had the Lord's favor, both material
and spiritual.

The children of Israel were showered with good things:

> For the Lord thy God bringeth thee into a good land, a
> land of brooks of water, of fountains and depths that spring
> out of valleys and hills; a land of wheat, and barley, and
> vines, and fig trees, and pomegranates, a land of oil olive, and
> honey; a land wherein thou shalt eat bread without scarce-
> ness, thou shalt not lack any thing in it; a land whose stones
> are iron, and out of whose hills thou mayest dig brass.
> When thou hast eaten and art full, then thou shalt bless the
> Lord thy God for the good land which he hath given thee.
> Beware that thou forget not the Lord thy God . . . and say
> in thine heart, My power and the might of mine hand hath
> gotten me this wealth. But thou shalt remember the Lord
> thy God: for it is he that giveth thee power to get wealth.
> — Deut. 8:7-18

From this we see the following: (1) God wanted them
to have the good things of life. (2) It was dependent upon
their keeping his commandments. (3) It was God who
gave them the power to get wealth. (4) He admonished
them not to forget him in their abundance.

*Do these Scriptures teach that all righteous people will
be rich?* No, but they do show that it is possible for a person
to be both righteous and rich. However, the Lord does promise material necessities to all who follow his commandments.
Christ promised: "Seek ye first the kingdom of God, and his
righteousness: and all these things shall be added unto you"
(Matt. 6:33), meaning the physical needs discussed in the
previous verses. How much — we do not know, but enough.

The Psalmist observed: "I have been young, and now am old; yet have I not seen the righteous forsaken, nor his seed begging bread" (Psa. 37:25). The person who begs bread does so because either he or someone else has failed to obey some of the Lord's commandments. How do we know this? Because God has given the instructions for obtaining life's needs, some of which are discussed in the following chapters.

Is it not possible for widows and others to be in need, even though they are righteous and God-fearing? Yes, but it still will not be necessary for them to beg bread, if God's will is followed. He has made provision for the needs of righteous widows. If they have been unable to make provision for their declining years, the Lord says their children are to care for them (I Tim. 5:4). The Christian widow who accepts help from a son or daughter is not a beggar. This is the Lord's provision under certain circumstances, and the son or daughter who shirks this responsibility has violated a positive commandment. The needy Christian widow who has no children is to be assisted by the church (I Tim. 5:16). This is not a matter of begging. If a widow must beg bread, it is proof that either she or others have failed in their sacred duties.

V. A SUMMARY OF OUR RELATIONSHIP TO MATERIAL THINGS.

When we think of Mary and Martha, one of the foremost things which comes to our minds is our constant relationship to the cares of the world and all material things attached to daily living. In this chapter and the following chapters, these principles are discussed:

God made material things for man's use and enjoyment (Chapter IV). But material prosperity is promised conditionally. We must do our part, if we expect the Lord to bless us. What does this involve?

All that we have should be used carefully and thriftily (Chapter V).

We must work. "Be thou diligent." "If any would not work, neither should he eat" (Chapter VI).

Possessions must be acquired honestly, used wisely, and occupy the proper place in our hearts, or they can cause us to lose our souls (Chapter VII).

Spiritual riches must always take precedence over material riches. The Lord should come first, as a prerequisite of both material and spiritual prosperity. "Honor the Lord with thy substance and with the firstfruits of all thine increase." "Seek ye first the kingdom of God" (Chapter VIII).

REVIEW EXERCISE

1. Quote a verse which states that we should enjoy God's blessings.

----

2. What promise is given to those who "honor the Lord with thy substance"? --

----

3. What promise is given to those who "bring ye all the tithes into the storehouse"? --

----

4. God "made the _____ and _____ _____ therein."

5. Name some of the good things of life which God placed here for our use --

----

6. Name some Biblical characters who were both rich and righteous --

----

7. Give two Scriptures which show that it is good to pray for success in every field of endeavor: (1)........................ (2)........................

8. What four principles are seen in a study of Deuteronomy 8:7-18?

....

....

9. What attitude should always accompany every prayer? ....

....

10. What will happen to "wealth gotten by vanity"? ....

11. God does not promise that everybody will be rich, but what does he promise to those who "seek first the kingdom of God?"........

....

12. What is the lesson taught in the Scripture which says, "Thou shalt not muzzle the ox that treadeth out the corn"?........................

....

13. Who is to care for needy widows? ....

14. Give the two commands, negative and positive, God has given in Ephesians 4:28 for obtaining material blessings. (1)............

.... (2) ....

....

FOR THOUGHT OR DISCUSSION

1. Though God promises to bless those who give to him (Mal. 3:10), do you think he will do so if this is the motive which prompts one to give?

2. Is it possible to become so self-satisfied with material gain that we tend to lose our perspective and to become unable to evaluate the really important issues of life? In such a case, what price tag has one put on his soul?

5.

"Gather Up the Fragments"

MARY and Martha had a house. It is spoken of as Martha's house. From this we would conclude that she owned a house and that she and her sister experienced all the problems and responsibilities which women today face in the managing of a home. This would include the matter of thrift and the careful use of all material things entrusted into our care. God's word has more to say on this subject than many have supposed. It involves sacred principles and duties.

Since God is the creator and giver of all material blessings, to waste material blessings is to waste the work of God. This is a very important lesson for all homemakers. It is estimated that women spend 80c of every dollar that is spent. This being true, women have heavy responsibilities to manage wisely and spend discriminately.

Thrift — many have confused it with stinginess or covetousness, but there is a definite distinction and a vast difference.

> Thrift is not wasting.
> Stinginess is not sharing.
>
> Thrift is preserving what you have.
> Covetousness is wanting what the other fellow has.

The Bible teaches thrift and condemns stinginess and covetousness.

I. BIBLICAL EXAMPLES OF THRIFT.

Christ taught against waste of material goods. On one occasion he fed five thousand people with five loaves and two fishes (Jno. 6:5-13). After everyone had finished eating, Jesus gave these instructions: "Gather up the fragments that remain, that nothing be lost." Why was he concerned about the food scraps? He had the ability to produce an unlimited amount of food, so why didn't he say, "Don't bother with the leftovers! there's plenty more where that came from"? Evidently he wanted his disciples to learn a lesson in economy. And that includes us.

Christ taught against waste. There are so many hungry and destitute people in the world that surely our conscience should smite us severely if we are guilty of wasting that which could be utilized either by us or someone else.

When God fed the children of Israel with manna from heaven, he gave them only a daily supply (Ex. 16:15-21). It was a perishable substance; and if he had showered them with more than they could use, some would have been wasted. Again we see the frugal use of material blessings.

God admonishes us to take a lesson from the ant: "Go to the ant, thou sluggard; consider her ways, and be wise: which having no guide, overseer, or ruler, provideth her meat in the summer, and gathereth her food in the harvest" (Prov. 6:6-8). Among other commendable qualities, the ant labors and saves a portion of the fruit of her labors for a leaner day. If she consumed or wasted all she could gather in the summer, she would perish in the winter snows.

This teaches the principle of consuming less than we produce — or in other words, of spending less than we earn. The person who never spends more than he earns will never find himself in need. So many are like the man who went to his friend and asked to borrow money. "You see," he explained, "I have been kind of over-supporting myself lately." The proverbial rainy day is sure to come; and if we have made no preparation for it, we have not wisely taken a lesson from the ant. "There is a treasure to be desired and oil in the dwelling of the wise; but a foolish man spendeth it up" (Prov. 21:20). The foolish person uses up all the oil with no thought for future needs; but the wise one saves enough to be prepared for tomorrow. The grasshopper philosophy of life will destroy us.

There is an admirable dignity attached to any home, however modest, which is living within its means. It escapes the harassment and pressure of unpaid bills and unbalanced budgets. On the other hand, extravagance by any member of a family can produce great frustration for the one who must pay the bills and often becomes a major cause of contention. Living within our income is a principle of God which promotes a sense of security and peace.

A lady from the city was talking to an old farmer and decrying the high cost of living. He smiled and said, "Lady, it ain't the high cost of living. It's the cost of folks living too high."

Joseph of Arimathea was a man whose material and financial planning enabled him to be of unusual service to his Lord. There was a need for a burial place for the body of Jesus. Joseph was ready to render this act of love. If he had not been thrifty, he would not have had a new tomb. Every act of benevolence must be rendered by someone who has not only worked but also been economical with the fruit of his labors.

The worthy woman described in Proverbs 31 "considereth a field and buyeth it" (ver. 16). If she had not been thrifty with her material goods, she would not have had enough left over to buy a field. The means of purchase had to come from somewhere. She could have chosen to spend all she made on silks and satins. feasting and fun, chariots or chariot-racing. But her frugality enabled her to invest in that which not only provided material security for herself and her family but also enabled her to stretch forth her hand to the poor (ver. 20) and in this way to be a blessing to others.

The New Testament teaches the same lesson. "Rather let him labor, working with his own hands the thing which is good, that he may have to give to him that needeth" (Eph. 4:28). It is good to be diligent and hard-working, but without wise management and economical use of that which is earned, we can have neither material security for ourselves nor the means of helping others. A fool may make money, but it needs a wise man to spend it.

The houses in which most people live are bought on credit. Have you ever stopped to think that this would be impossible if somebody somewhere had not practiced thrift? The bank or individual who finances the purchase of homes on credit must do so on someone's savings. Thus, every person who is buying a home on credit is enjoying the fruits of someone else's work and thrift. This would not be possible if everyone either spent or wasted everything he made each week.

The one-talent man was rebuked severely (Matt. 25:14-30). What had he done? He had wasted the earning power of the money entrusted to him. The wise woman described in Proverbs 31 had invested in a field. The one-talent man failed to do this. He did not deliberately destroy the one talent, but he failed to put it to that use which would increase it.

II. WHAT THRIFT REQUIRES.

A wise use of material possessions is something which must be learned. What does it require?

Maturity. We need to grow up. Paul said, "When I was a child, I spake as a child, I understood as a child, I thought as a child: but when I became a man, I put away childish things" (I Cor. 13:11). Self-discipline is a part of maturity. The person who cannot discipline self has never grown up. We must be able to forego today's wants in view of tomorrow's needs. A child is unable to do this. He gets whatever he wants, if he can, with no thought of the future. We must learn to control our material wants, rather than let our wants control us.

Managerial qualities. God intended for man to be master over material things. When he placed Adam in Eden, he instructed him to subdue the earth and have dominion over all things therein. This required the ability of management. Animals do not have this power; this is a duty enjoined upon man alone.

It has been said that the average American housewife throws out approximately one-seventh of all groceries bought. This may not be true of you, but it gives us something to think about. In such a case, think what good could be done if one-seventh of everyone's weekly grocery bill could be channeled into better and wiser use than consignment to a garbage can. You have heard it said that a woman can throw more out the back door than a man can bring in the front door. This is almost literally true. It takes far more wisdom to manage money than to make it.

Thrift is a household mint. The best source of wealth is economy. It is surely true that a dollar saved is a dollar earned. No matter how much one may produce, he can never have wealth without economy. Wise management would enable many people to have more than they do. All who have had much experience in helping needy people have had the sad experience of taking clothing to a destitute family, only to return later and find the clothing on the floor being walked on. It was not a matter of not having. It was a case of improper management of what they had. That same lack of management was one cause of their plight in the first place. "Willful waste makes woeful want." Even if we had not witnessed it, God tells us this: "He becometh poor that dealeth with a slack hand" (Prov. 10:4).

In a family, thrift requires teamwork and cooperation. If one is thrifty and the other a spendthrift, a problem is ever-present. Since the making and use of money is an inescapable responsibility of each family, it can easily become the means of dissension.

Thrift requires planning. It never comes accidentally. Some families never sit down together and make any financial plans. They simply spend whatever they can on that which is the most urgent or desirable at the time. Planning necessitates teamwork, as mentioned above. No matter how hard one person in the family may work toward financial security and careful planning, these plans cannot be carried out without the cooperation of the whole family.

Sometimes people can be as short-sighted and shallow in their planning as the woman who was trying to get her husband to buy a new car. "But how will we pay for it?" he asked. She said: "Now let's not confuse the issue by considering two problems at the same time."

III. PITFALLS TO WATCH IN PRACTICING THRIFT.

Every good thing can be perverted and made to become a liability. Therefore, it is highly appropriate to call attention to some of the perversions which can grow from an improper understanding and practice of a God-given commandment.

Selfishness can result. One can become so concerned over the frugal use of material possessions that his heart may be closed to the needs of others. If so, this becomes a perversion of God's law, rather than obedience to a divine command. May we never violate Philippians 2:4.

Stinginess may develop if the desire to practice economy is carried too far. It can be carried as far as the Scotch proprietor who posted a sign over the clock in the lobby of his hotel: "For the use of guests only." The stingy heart has lost sight of the very spirit of Christianity.

One may rob God because of a mistaken idea of his responsibility to be frugal (Mal. 3:8,9). The same God who teaches thrift in material matters also teaches generosity toward himself and mankind. These two commands are not in conflict. As already discussed, the thrifty person is one who plans and wisely spends on his own needs in order that he may have to give to God and others. It was said of a certain Christian man that he would walk a mile to save a dime, and then when he got there he would give generously to any good cause. Thrift will enable us to give more to the Lord's cause, but some have allowed their frugality to lead them to slight God.

In an effort to practice economical use of material things, *one may over-value them in proportion to spiritual things* (I Tim. 6:9,10).

There is such a thing as false economy. When Mary poured the valuable ointment on the feet of Jesus, the disciples standing around thought the ointment was wasted (Jno. 12:3-5). They had a false idea of economy. They rebuked her and suggested that the ointment could have been sold and the money given to the poor. Jesus in turn rebuked them for their lack of understanding. That which is given into the service of our Master is never wasted.

REVIEW EXERCISE

1. What is the difference between thrift and stinginess? _____

_____

2. What is the difference between thrift and covetousness?..............

----

3. What good deed was done by Joseph of Arimathea? ....

4. How did Christ teach a lesson on thrift?.......................................

----

5. What did the one-talent man do with that which was entrusted to him? ....

6. How does the ant teach a lesson on thrift? ....

----

7. (T or F) Christ had no interest in what people did with their material things.

8. (T or F) Thrift will enable us to do more to help other people.

9. List the pitfalls one must watch lest he develop a perverted idea of thrift. ....

----

10. What indicates that the woman described in Proverbs 31 was a good and thrifty manager? ....

11. What reason for working is given in Ephesians 4:28? ....

----

12. Who had a false idea of economy?......................Scripture:..........

13. What is one mark of maturity necessary to practice of thrift?........

FOR THOUGHT OR DISCUSSION

1. Discuss some ways the average family may be guilty of wasting (1) food, (2) clothing, (3) other material things in the home.

2. A Christian woman whose non-Christian husband objected to her

giving anything to the Lord said she overcame the problem by better home management. For example: one day each week she served beans instead of steak and gave the saving to the Lord. By cutting other corners, she obeyed God's command to give and yet managed the home in a manner pleasing to her husband.

6.

"If Any Would Not Work"

GOD intends for us to enjoy the fruit of our labor, but the fruit was never promised apart from the labor. We are living in an age when so many want to reap all the blessings of work without doing anything; at least, without doing very much. Some are like the little boy who knocked at the door of a spacious house and asked for yard work. The household was already well supplied with servants, and the lady said, "I am sorry, but we already have one yard boy, and we really don't have enough work to keep two boys busy." "Lady," said the boy, "You must have! You just don't know what a little amount of work it takes to keep me busy!"

> He is not worthy of the honeycomb
> That shuns the hive because the bees have stings.
>
> — Shakespeare

I. WORK IS A SACRED RESPONSIBILITY.

God and Christ set the example. "My Father worketh hitherto, and I work" (Jno. 5:17).

The Lord has much to say on this subject, and says some very hard things about those who will not work. "If any would not work, neither should he eat" (II Thess. 3:10). This is awfully plain preaching! And not at all popular.

In strong and unmistakable terms, the Lord further says: "If any provide not for their own, and specially for those of his own house, he hath denied the faith, and is worse than an infidel" (I Tim. 5:8).

II. THE CONDITIONAL PROMISES OF GOD.

Though God sends rain on the just and the unjust, there are certain conditions with which man must comply if he would enjoy material prosperity, just as there are conditions of spiritual prosperity. If man fails to meet the conditions, he will not succeed. One of these conditions is a willingness to work.

"Be thou diligent to know the state of thy flocks, and look well to thy herds . . . The lambs are for thy clothing and the goats are the price of the field. And thou shalt have goats' milk enough for thy food" (Prov. 27:23-27). The clothing was not promised without work, and the milk was not enjoyed without effort. "Be thou diligent." Diligence involves work, but it includes more. The dictionary defines diligence: "Assiduous and constant application to one's business or duty; careful and persevering effort to accomplish what is undertaken; industry."

The worthy woman described in Proverbs 31 was showered with material and spiritual prosperity, but such was not miraculously dropped down on her out of heaven. She "worketh willingly," and "eateth not the bread of idleness." It almost makes your back ache just to read of all her work; but such was the prerequisite of the abundant spiritual and material living she enjoyed. Surely she lived the good life. She had the favor of God; her husband and children loved and lauded her; she was known and praised at the gates of the city; she enjoyed the tapestry, silk, purple and fine linen which is a joy to the heart of women appreciative of beauty. Was it that her husband was a good provider who showered her with all the luxuries of life? We are told nothing of his labors, though surely we learn from other Scriptures that he also had a responsibility to work and to provide for his family; but the point we are giving here is that the woman was willing to work hard and manage wisely for the sake of her family.

> She seeketh wool, and flax, and worketh willingly with her hands . . . bringeth her food from afar . . . riseth also while it is yet night, and giveth meat to her household and a portion to her maidens . . . with the fruit of her hands she planteth a vineyard . . . layeth her hands to the spindle, and her hands to the distaff . . . stretcheth out her hand to the poor; yea, she reacheth forth her hands to the needy . . . all her household are clothed with scarlet; she maketh herself coverings of tapestry; her clothing is silk, and purple . . . looketh well to the ways of her household, and eateth not the bread of idleness. — Prov. 31:13-27

The worthy woman was diligent not only in physical labors, but also in spiritual attainments. It takes effort. This is the meaning of II Timothy 2:15: "Study [give diligence, A.S.V.] to show thyself approved unto God, a workman that needeth not to be ashamed, rightly dividing the word of truth." It includes much more than just reading or studying God's word. It means to work diligently toward spiritual attainment, whatever that entails, so that one may be approved in God's sight. One day a little elderly lady called the church office and told of some church work she had just completed. Then she said: "I've decided that if you want the Lord to know that you're around, you have to do something to attract his attention."

Surely all of us would like to enjoy the life of the worthy woman, but are we willing to put forth as much effort as she did?

"Let him that stole steal no more: but rather let him labor, *working with his hands the thing which is good,* that he may have to give to him that needeth" (Eph. 4:28). The having is preceded by the working.

"*In all labor there is profit:* but the talk of the lips tendeth only to penury" (Prov. 14:23). The profit is to be preceded by the labor. Penury means destitution or extreme poverty. The person who wants to do all talking and no working ends in poverty and then wonders why. It is because he has failed to follow God's law of industry, for we are to be "not slothful in business" (Rom. 12:11). Poverty is not disgraceful in itself, but it is when it stems from idleness, slothfulness, intemperance or extravagance.

"The soul of the sluggard desireth, but hath nothing: *but the soul of the diligent shall be made fat*" (Prov. 13:4). Note the condition upon which the blessing hinges.

"Seest thou a man diligent in his business? He shall stand before kings; he shall not stand before mean men" (Prov. 22:29). The recognition is conditional. An ambitious young man asked a great merchant to reveal the secret of success. The man answered: "Just jump at your opportunity." "But how can I tell when my opportunity is coming?" asked the young man. "You can't," replied the merchant; "just keep watching."

III. WHY HAS GOD ORDAINED WORK?

Many regard work as a curse upon mankind and feel that the ability to get out of it is one of man's shrewdest attainments. It is true that sin added burdens to work, but work itself had previously been ordained by God. When he placed Adam and Eve in Eden he commanded them to dress and keep the garden. This provision was made by a loving Father for the benefit of mankind. What good purposes are served by work?

Human energy is one of the necessary means of production, and without its use man cannot enjoy the blessings intended for him by his Creator. For instance, God has provided seed, but man must expend the effort of planting and harvesting, or he does not receive the blessing. Human energy is necessary to convert the trees of the forest into homes for man's enjoyment. This list could be multiplied manyfold, and we can see why God commanded work. It was for the good of all society.

Our efforts bless not only ourselves, but are necessary if we are to help others (Eph. 4:28). The selfish person thinks only of the work he can avoid; the unselfish one thinks of what he can do to make life more pleasant or lighten the load for someone else — and this involves effort. When Jesus gave the formula for true greatness he said: "But he that is greatest among you shall be your servant" (Matt. 23:11). "Your servant." This means work, and many people are just too lazy to be great. They want greatness draped over them like a cloak, without any effort on their part, but it doesn't come this way. The willing horse is given the hardest jobs, but he is also given the most hay.

Work is a blessing because idleness leads to many ills. We have observed this, even if God had not told us; but he understood this principle from the beginning and warned against this pitfall: "And withal they learn to be idle, wandering about from house to house; and not only idle, but tattlers also and busybodies, speaking things which they ought not" (I Tim. 5:13). From childhood you have heard that "an idle mind is the devil's workshop." It has always been so, and it still is. Minds cannot be a vacuum. They are filled with something, and therefore we see God's wisdom in ordaining that we stay busy with worthwhile endeavors.

IV. WHAT SLOTHFULNESS WILL DO.

We can further see the blessing of work when we examine what slothfulness will do to ourselves and to all society.

It will lead to poverty. "He becometh poor that dealeth

with a slack hand; but the hand of the diligent maketh rich"
(Prov. 10:4). "How long wilt thou sleep, O sluggard? when
wilt thou arise out of thy sleep? Yet a little sleep, a little
slumber, a little folding of the hands to sleep. So shall thy
poverty come as one that traveleth, and thy want as an armed
man" (Prov. 6:6-11). Poverty came. But why? He loved
sleep too much. "The sluggard will not plow by reason of the
cold; therefore shall he beg in harvest, and have nothing"
(Prov. 20:4). A beggar. Why? Because he was too lazy
to plow when it was cold.

"As the door turneth upon his hinges, so doth the slothful
upon his bed. The slothful hideth his hand in his bosom;
it grieveth him to bring it out again" (Prov. 26:14.15). Can
you imagine a more graphic description of extreme laziness?
"The slothful man saith, There is a lion in the way; a lion is
in the streets" (Prov. 26:13). Of course, this was just an
excuse. When a person does not want to work, it is easy
to begin to make excuses. This is true concerning everything, as illustrated in the story which has been told concerning two Arabs. One went to his friend and said: "I want to
borrow your rope." The friend said, "I can't let you have it;
I need it to tie up my milk." The startled Arab said. "Why,
you can't tie milk with a rope." "I know it," said the friend,
"But when you don't want to do something, one excuse is as
good as another."

Sometimes diligent and hard-working people find themselves in temporary need because of a combination of circumstances beyond their control; but these Scriptures teach that
the most prevalent cause of destitute conditions is simply a
failure to put out the required effort. A business man has a
placard in his office which says: "I fight poverty. I work."

Slothfulness is a waste and misuse of energy and talent.
As already mentioned, human energy is one of the necessary

means of production. Without it, nothing can be produced; and laziness is a desecration of that power which God has placed in us. The one-talent man idled away his time, refused to expend any energy and thus buried his talent. He was condemned for it (Matt. 25:30). "He also that is slothful in his work is brother to him that is a great waster" (Prov. 18:9). He is wasting, not material goods, but energy which could be converted into attainment.

Laziness can cause deterioration in what we have. "I went by the field of the slothful, and by the vineyard of the man void of understanding; and, lo, it was grown over with thorns, and nettles had covered the face thereof, and the stone wall thereof was broken down. Then I saw, and considered it well: I looked upon it, and received instruction" (Prov. 24:30-32). "By much slothfulness the building decayeth; and through idleness of the hands the house droppeth through" (Eccl. 10:18). One way to have more is to take better care of what we have. Without effort in preserving those things we have, they will soon deteriorate and we will find ourselves in need.

One who will not work forfeits his own right to the material blessings of life. This is made plain in our text: "If any would not work, neither should he eat." It is not true that the world owes us a living. The world was here first. It owes us nothing.

Slothfulness is actually theft, for the lazy person who goes through life refusing to carry his part of the load is living off the labors of other people. He is taking that which he has not earned, just as surely as the person who robs a bank. He wants something for nothing, but nothing is free. Somebody has to expend the effort to provide, or there would never be clothing to wear or food to eat or cars to drive.

Our nation has almost lost sight of this principle, though it is one of the basic ones upon which our country was founded. The story has been told of a king who called upon his economic advisors to prepare a paper on economics which he planned to use to develop a strong and prosperous people. The advisors spent several months on the assignment and finally came back with ten volumes on the subject. It was too long and too deep for the average citizen, so the king dismissed all the experts except five and charged them to make the report shorter and simpler. They came back with a hundred page volume on economics. The king demanded that the report be simpler and shorter. His economic experts worked and worked and finally came back with two quotations from the Bible: "If any would not work, neither should he eat." "Gather up the fragments."

It matters not how many deadheads ride free of charge, somebody has to pay the freight. It may be considered smart to ride free of charge, but one who goes through life doing so is actually stealing from the labors of others. "The slothful man roasteth not that which he took in hunting" (Prov. 12:27). He liked to hunt, but he didn't like to roast; and it is implied that he well may have starved if someone else had not been willing to do the roasting for him.

V. WHAT IS OUR ATTITUDE TOWARD OUR DUTIES?

The worthy woman "worketh willingly" (Prov. 31:13). The first word tells what she did. The second word describes her attitude and disposition while she was doing it. Have you ever known a woman who would sweep, mop, wash and iron — but try to make her family feel that she was a mistreated and overworked slave? She obeyed the command to work, but she erred by having an ungodly attitude toward work.

This one point can sometimes make the difference between a home that is filled with harmony and contentment and a home filled with discord and resentment. The woman who constantly murmurs about all the things she has to do makes herself and her family miserable. A cheerful attitude in discharging our duties will furnish a tonic for everyone in the household. An invalid woman advertised for a housekeeper, asking for "a cheerful Christian, if possible."

May we "do all things without murmurings and disputings" (Phil 2:14), and develop the attitude and habit of working willingly — for an unwilling and complaining attitude is a habit which one may drift into without realizing it.

"Whatsoever thy hand findeth to do, do it with thy might" (Eccl. 9:10).

REVIEW EXERCISE

1. What adverb especially describes the work of the worthy woman in Proverbs 31? _____

2. "Be thou _____ to _____ the state of thy flocks." Scripture: _____

3. How can one who believes in God be worse than an infidel? _____ ___ _____

4. (T or F) Christ stated that the Father worketh.

5. At what time did the worthy woman in Proverbs 31 arise?_____ _____

6. Just the talk of the lips tends only to _____

7. Jesus' formula for greatness consisted of _____

8. Who desires but does not have?_____ Scripture:_____

9. (T or F) It takes a certain kind of hand to avoid poverty and to gather material blessings.

10. What sins are mentioned in I Timothy 5:13 fostered by idleness?

11. What does the slothful man say about a lion? ....

                                   Scripture: ....

12. The property of the slothful is described as ....

                            (Prov. 24:30-32) and ....

                                       (Eccl. 10:18).

13. Whatever your hand finds to do, you should do it with your............

14. How does the slothful turn upon his bed? ....

FOR THOUGHT OR DISCUSSION

1. Some women have admitted that it is difficult for them to "work willingly" while their husbands rest, read or watch television. Discuss some principles which apply in such a situation. Is it not true that most men are carrying heavy loads of responsibility, and willingly?

2. Discuss some practical ways whereby care and work can preserve material things and enable us to have more.

7.

"It Is Easier For A Camel"

THOUGH God created material things for man's use and enjoyment, every good thing can be misappropriated; and for this reason very strong warnings are given concerning some of the possible pitfalls in connection with possessions.

Jesus told of a rich young man whose wealth had become a snare to his soul. Then he concluded: "It is easier for a camel to go through the eye of a needle, than for a rich man to enter into the kingdom of God" (Matt. 19:24). What did Jesus mean? Did he place a curse upon all riches? Does this verse contradict all the other Scriptures we have studied? Of course not. The passage must be understood in harmony with all other teachings on the same subject. Various efforts have been made to explain this verse. Some have suggested that the needle was a gate near Jerusalem, a difficult passageway for a camel. However, it seems more logical that Christ was simply using a proverbial expression with which his hearers were familiar, a hyperbole, to denote a thing very difficult or impossible. Such expressions are found in literature of other nations, some using other animals such as the elephant to express the same thought.

Christ's words so startled his disciples that "they were exceedingly amazed, saying, *Who then can be saved?*" They understood that if Christ meant this literally and absolutely, no person could be saved. We must understand that it is a relative expression, for several reasons: (1) God tells of men who were godly and wealthy, and thus we know that such can be saved. (2) Riches are relative. Who is rich? To the average person, it is anyone who has more than he has. When compared to the starving throngs of India and other nations, every American is rich. Can any American be saved? Who is going to set the standard of who is rich and who is poor? (3) In verse 26 of the same passage, Jesus further states: "With men this is impossible; but with God all things are possible." He clearly affirms that he is talking about an impossible thing if it were dependent upon man's ability; then he clarifies the teaching by saying that the thing which is impossible for man is possible with God. Men, by their own power and strength, cannot save themselves from the snare of riches, or anything else, but with God's help all things are possible.

Our Lord gave the real explanation when he discussed the rich fool and then concluded: "So is he that layeth up treasure for himself, and is not rich toward God" (Lk. 12:21). His sin was not in his wealth, but in the fact that he was not rich toward God. He was a spiritual pauper.

Though wealth can be used to bless mankind and to promote the work of God, it can also destroy man's soul. Therefore, we must consider the various sins into which one may fall.

I. ACQUIRING WEALTH DISHONESTLY.

Many sin by acquiring wealth dishonestly in a manner which robs or harms another. "Provide things honest in the sight of all men" (Rom. 12:17). Today the increase of wealth by lying is a practice so common that many business men feel they could not make a living if they were truthful about all goods and services with which they deal. The Lord says such a practice will bring destruction finally. "The getting of treasures by a lying tongue is a vanity tossed to and fro of them that seek death. The robbery of the wicked shall destroy them; because they refuse to do judgment" (Prov.

21:6,7). "He that is greedy of gain troubleth his own house" (Prov. 15:27).

Such greed of gain has caused some to commit murder (Prov. 1:18,19). Riches mean more to some people than life itself.

Greed has caused others to defraud and mistreat those who work for them: "Go to now, ye rich men, weep and howl for your miseries that shall come upon you. Your riches are corrupted, and your garments are moth-eaten. Your gold and silver is cankered; and the rust of them shall be a witness against you" (Jas. 5:1-3). What was their sin? The Lord explains it: "Behold; the hire of the laborers who have reaped down your fields, which is of you kept back by fraud, crieth: and the cries of them which have reaped are entered into the ears of the Lord of Sabaoth" (Jas. 5:4). They had acquired riches by defrauding their fellowman.

II. MATERIAL PROSPERITY HAS CAUSED SOME TO FORGET GOD.

The comforts which come with plenty tend to make some people feel less need of God. This is what happened to the children of Israel. After God had blessed them immeasurably and brought them safely into the land of Canaan, they turned away from him in their prosperity, ease and pleasure. They forgot to give him credit for all their blessings.

A preacher visited a prosperous farmer, intending to talk with him about contributing to a worthy cause. As they looked over the bountiful crops, the preacher said, "The Lord has been so good to you. Just look at all the blessings he has bestowed upon you." The farmer snapped: "The Lord had nothing to do with it. I'm the one who made these crops." Oh, blindness! how blind thou art! What could he have done without the Lord's sunshine, soil, rain and the germ of life within the planted seed? Yes, he had forgotten that it was God who gave him the power to acquire his possessions. Men sometimes want to credit themselves with all their successes and the Lord with all their failures.

The dangers inherent in both poverty and wealth were recognized by the sacred writer: "Give me neither poverty nor riches . . . lest I be full, and deny thee . . . or lest I be poor, and steal, and take the name of my God in vain" (Prov. 30:7-9).

III. WEALTH HAS CAUSED SOME TO BE HIGH-MINDED.

This pitfall is discussed in God's word: "Charge them that are rich in this world, that they be not high-minded" (I Tim. 6:17).

The world has a tendency to judge people by what they have, instead of by what they are. Consequently, it becomes easy for the wealthy person to become filled with pride, to think he *is* something merely because he *has* something. Pride, or high-mindedness, is one of the strongest bars against entrance into the kingdom of heaven. To enter the Lord's kingdom, which is his church, one must be willing to submit himself humbly and completely to the will of God (Jno. 5:30). If one has allowed wealth or worldly acclaim to puff him up with high-mindedness, he is unable to do this and therefore remains outside the kingdom of heaven.

The rich may sin in their high-mindedness, and others may sin in their attitude toward the rich. There are two ways in which people sin relatively to the wealthy: (1) *One is respect.* Some look up to the wealthy merely because of their riches, catering to them and condoning their actions in order to stay on their good side. God tells of some Christians who sinned in this way: "For if there come unto your assembly a man with a gold ring, in goodly apparel, and there come in also a poor man in vile raiment; and he have respect to him that weareth the gay clothing, and say unto him, Sit thou here in a good place; and say to the poor, Stand thou there, or sit here under my footstool . . . but if ye have respect of persons, ye commit sin, and are convinced of the law as transgressors" (Jas. 2:2-9). (2) *Another sinful attitude is disrespect.* Some look down on all wealthy persons, condemning them and regarding them as evil merely because of their possessions. Both attitudes, either undue respect or disrespect, are out of harmony with God's will.

IV. ANOTHER SIN IS TRUSTING IN RICHES.

"Charge them that are rich in this world, that they be not high-minded, nor trust in uncertain riches" (I Tim. 6:17).

How does one trust in riches? Because money can buy so many things and wield so much influence in this world, one may feel that with it he can do all things and thus has no need of God. It comes as a real shock to some people the first time they face a serious problem which money will not cure — such as sickness and death. It will not buy a ticket at the gate of heaven. Therefore, "If riches increase, set not your heart upon them" (Psa. 62:10).

It is foolish to trust in riches because of their transitory nature. They may be snatched away overnight. "Riches certainly make themselves wings; they fly away as an eagle toward heaven" (Prov. 23:5). No matter what we have, it can never buy the most important things in this life; and, furthermore, what it can buy must be left behind at the grave. "For he seeth that wise men die, likewise the fool and the brutish person, and leave their wealth to others" (Prov. 49:10).

It is likewise foolish to trust in riches because of their deceitful nature (Matt. 13:22). Wealth holds before its would-be procurers glowing promises of happiness and satisfaction, promises which it cannot fulfill. Yet many, like Solomon, have followed its vain and empty promises to the bitter end, only to conclude in heartache and despair: "All is vanity and vexation of the spirit."

V. THE LOVE OF MONEY IS SINFUL.

"The love of money is the root of all evil" (I Tim. 6:10). This is one of the most misquoted passages in the Bible. It does not say: "Money is the root of all evil." It is the love of money that is condemned, and this sin is committed by many who have little. It is possible to have money without loving it. Abraham did, for the Lord was the first love of his heart and he is called the father of the faithful and a friend of God. It is also possible to love money without having it. Judas did, and it caused him to betray his Lord. Judas sold out for thirty pieces of silver (Matt. 27:3-9). A good question for each is: Do I have a price? Many who have not quit the fellowship of the church have made some very grievous mistakes because money was involved. Its power is great. It may influence some church leaders who are anxious to build up their own private businesses to pursue a soft line in dealing with worldly and disorderly members. If we were to take away two loves — love of money and love of human praise — and add one — love of God — it would be much easier to handle the problems which arise in church work; and wherever you have people you will have problems.

It is not money but the love of it which leads to some of the other sins we are discussing: lying, stealing, defrauding, murder, envy and covetousness. The rich young ruler loved his possessions so much they had become the idol of his heart (Matt. 19:16-26). It was not his wealth that condemned him, but his love of it.

The love of possessions is an insatiable thing. The more one has, the more one wants, if this is the love of his heart. "He that loveth silver shall not be satisfied with silver; nor he that loveth abundance with increase" (Eccl. 5:10-13).

VI. A FAILURE TO USE WEALTH PROPERLY.

One may actually rob God by refusing to give to his work (Mal. 3:8). God has always taught man to give in proportion to what he makes (I Cor. 16:2). A failure to do this is sinful, a robbery of God.

A failure to help others is also sinful. "But whoso hath this world's good, and seeth his brother have need, and shutteth his bowels of compassion from him, how dwelleth the love of God in him?" (I Jno. 3:17).

VII. COVETOUSNESS AND ENVY ARE SINS RELATED TO MATERIAL THINGS.

These sins often involve possessions, though not restricted to such. Covetousness and envy are related, and yet different. Covetousness is "being very desirous, especially of another's property; grasping; avaricious." Envy is "a feeling of chagrine or unhappiness over the good fortune or accomplishment of another." One may be guilty of envy without coveting what another has. For instance: Suppose Mrs. A has a purple Model-T car. Mrs. B probably would not want it at all! But if she is unhappy and upset because Mrs. A has it, that is envy.

Suppose Mr. C is a U. S. Senator. It may be that his longtime friend, Mr. D, would not under any circumstances want to be a senator; but if he is pained over Senator C's attainment, that is envy.

Suppose Mrs. E and her family buy a new home and her friend, Mrs. F, is so distressed over this good fortune that she is unable to "rejoice with them that rejoice." Then Mrs. F is guilty of the sin of envy.

One good definition of a friend is: one who likes you in spite of your achievements.

Think how many times the sin of envy is related to material things; and the sin is more prevalent among poor than among the rich. Therefore, no one escapes the possibility of sin with reference to materialism. Envy is listed in the catalog of some of the blackest sins (Gal. 5:19-21). God calls it what it is: rottenness, the "rottenness of the bones" (Prov. 14:30). It acts on one's heart and gradually destroys it.

VIII. CONCLUSION.

In view of so many possibilities of sin in connection with wealth, would it be better to have nothing? Of course not. This would not insure one against sin. In the first place, our relationship to material things is inescapable, constant and necessary. In the next place, it is possible for one who has very little to sin with reference to riches and lose his soul, just as it is for the wealthy. Nearly all who are not rich are hoping and struggling to increase what they have, and thus Christ's warning applies to them also.

A person's relationship to God is determined by his heart, not his bank account. Therefore, we have seen the rich who like Abraham and Job, were also rich in faith and good works. Then we have seen the very poor who were guilty of envy, covetousness, the love of wealth, and dishonesty in their struggle to acquire more and more. "But with God all things are possible." Only through his help and keeping our affections set on things above can any person win the battle against materialism, whether he be rich or poor.

REVIEW EXERCISE

1. "Provide things _____ in the sight of all _____."

    Scripture: _____

2. (T or F) Christ taught that a camel can go through the eye of a needle.

3. What does the greedy person do to his own house? _____

4. What charge did Paul want made to those who "are rich in this world"? _____

_____

5. Jesus said that the person who is rich in this world's goods but poor toward God is _____

6. What sin of partiality did James mention that church leaders may be tempted to commit? _____

_____

7. What internal trouble does envy indicate? _____

8. Where did the cries of some defrauded people enter? _____

_____

9. What was the witness against some rich men? _____

10. "If riches increase, set not _____ "

   Scripture:_____

11. What is the root of all evil? _____

12. (T or F) The Bible teaches that one can make enough money to become satisfied with it.

13. (T or F) People 1900 years ago had no gold and silver.

FOR THOUGHT OR DISCUSSION

1. Consider the dangers inherent in both poverty and wealth as taught in Proverbs 30:7-9 and also discuss additional dangers in both which may not have been brought out in the lesson.

2. If one should look up to us merely because of what we have, or look down on us because of what we don't have, is that person worthy of our friendship at all?

8.

Choosing The Good Part

WE have sacred responsibilities in two realms, the material and the spiritual, and we must learn to blend these in a manner acceptable to God. Every day is a series of decisions. Some concern material duties; others involve spiritual responsibilities. At times these spheres seem to conflict and we are faced with choosing, with making another decision. Let's consider some principles which can guide us.

I. THE INTERWEAVING OF MATERIAL AND SPIRITUAL DUTIES.

Some think of religion as something tacked onto the rest of life, a vague spiritual matter far removed from daily chores and cares. Nothing could be further from the truth. Christianity is the daily and constant penetrating of God's will through every thought and deed. It is the breathing of an eternal force through a temporal world. From some viewpoints it is not possible to completely separate the material and spiritual aspects of our lives.

Making a living is a part of God's law and therefore is good, not evil. The man who refuses to do so has "denied the faith and is worse than an infidel" (I Tim. 5:8). Abiding in the faith includes material work. Therefore, the man who is busy making a living for his family is not violating God's law but is living within a part of it. However, if he centers his life around this to the exclusion of other divine commandments, he will lose his soul just as the rich fool did (Lk. 12:19-21).

One who keeps a house does so by the authority of the Lord, and the woman who rejects this responsibility blasphemes the word of God (Tit. 2:5). Therefore, the one who sweeps, mops, irons and cooks is not neglecting God's law; she is living within that specified part of it. She errs only when these duties become the whole life to the neglect of other precepts of God.

Feeding and clothing the needy, visiting the sick and befriending the stranger will be brought up at the judgment day (Matt. 25:35-46). These involve material things; yet they are spiritual works, for Christ said, "Ye did it unto me." The Good Samaritan engaged in physical works — bound up wounds, poured in wine and oil, paid the innkeeper — but these acts were only evidence of the spiritual quality of mercy (Lk. 10:30-37). The person engaged in these works has not forgotten God's law; he is living within a command of it. He errs, however, if he assumes that these works of goodness constitute the whole of his duties toward God. Some have done this and are depending upon these things to take them to heaven.

Spending some time in sleep and rest is a part of God's law. Our bodies were made to require rest. Christ felt this need. In resting he was not forgetting God's law; he was abiding by it. Even this, however, can become wrong when carried to excess.

Man needs not only rest but diversion which will recreate his lagging spirit; thus, we see Christ participating in a wedding feast. He was not temporarily unmindful of the Father's will; he was living within a part of it. We see again the inter-relationship of physical and spiritual activities, but we sin if life is centered around social activities to the neglect of the whole of God's law.

By giving of material treasures, Mary showed her supreme devotion to Christ. This is vividly portrayed in a touching scene recorded in John 12:1-9. Mary and Martha had prepared a supper for Jesus. Lazarus and others were there. "Then took Mary a pound of ointment of spikenard, very costly, and anointed the feet of Jesus, and wiped his feet with her hair." Judas rebuked her, implying extravagance, and suggested that the ointment could have been sold to help the poor. "Then Jesus said, Let her alone: against the day of my burying hath she kept this." This is one of the loneliest sentences in the Bible. Jesus knew that he was soon to die, and Mary was actually anointing him for the burial. Love, which is a spiritual quality, found expression in that which was material.

This is still true today. We are commanded to give (I Cor. 16:2). This involves the material, but it is actually an expression of our love for the Lord. It is possible to give without loving, but it is not possible to love without giving. Again we see the interweaving of our spiritual and material duties.

"Present your bodies a living sacrifice, holy, acceptable unto God, which is your reasonable [spiritual, A.S.V.] service" (Rom. 12:1). This involves physical and material aspects of life which cannot be separated from the spiritual law of God. The use of the body testifies to the spiritual status of the heart; because in the heart every deed, word and activity of life originates.

This principle is summed up in Colossians 3:17: "Whatsoever ye do in word or deed, do all in the name of the Lord." "Word or deed." This includes everything. "In the name of the Lord." This means by the authority of the Lord. For example, if a policeman knocks on your door and says: "Open up, in the name of the law," he means by the authority of the law. Thus, all activities of life, both spiritual and material, should be controlled by the law of God. "Whether therefore ye eat, or drink, or whatsoever ye do, do all to the glory of God" (I Cor. 10:31). "Whatsoever ye do." This includes every sphere of life.

MARTHA OR MARY?

I cannot choose; I should have liked so much
To sit at Jesus' feet — to feel the touch
Of his kind gentle hand upon my head
While drinking in the gracious words he said.

And yet to serve Him! Oh, divine employ —
To minister and give the Master joy;
To bathe in coolest springs his weary feet,
And wait upon Him while He sat at meat!

Worship or service — which? Ah, that is best
To which he calls us, be it toil or rest;
To labor for Him in life's busy stir,
Or seek His feet, a silent worshiper.

— Caroline Atherton Mason

II. "THAT GOOD PART, WHICH SHALL NOT BE TAKEN AWAY."

Though there is a close interweaving of material and spiritual duties, *Christ taught that at times a distinction must be made and the spiritual aspect must always take precedence.* "And she had a sister called Mary, who also sat at Jesus' feet, and heard his word. But Martha was cumbered about much serving, and came to him, and said, Lord, dost thou not care that my sister hath left me to serve alone? bid her therefore that she help me. And Jesus answered and said unto her, Martha, Martha, thou art careful and troubled about many things: But one thing is needful; and Mary hath chosen that good part, which shall not be taken away from her" (Lk. 10:38-42).

For what did Christ rebuke Martha? It was not for cooking a meal. He chided her only after she placed too much emphasis on the secondary aspects of life. She became so tense and anxious over daily household duties that the more important spiritual opportunities were temporarily crowded from her mind. Within itself, preparing a meal was not evil, but good. What would Christ, Paul, Timothy and all other gospel preachers have done without good women who were willing to cook and iron and care for all other physical needs so they could devote their time to spreading the Word? Christ understood this, and Marthas are needed; but the Marthas also need to be reminded that these good and necessary duties are always secondary to our spiritual responsibilities. They are a means of promoting something greater.

Christ said, "But one thing is needful." All of us have a deep-rooted feeling that there must be one great single purpose to life, but many go through this world confused and wondering what that one thing is. Some have looked for it in material success, social prestige or attainment in the arts and sciences, only to be disillusioned and disappointed. Our Lord defines life's single purpose: to choose that "which shall not be taken away" from us. "For we brought nothing into this world, and it is certain we can carry nothing out" (I Tim. 6:7). At death we will be separated from all material things. What "shall not be taken away"? Only the soul. Therefore, the "good part" of life is that which goes into preparing the immortal soul for eternity — worship, prayer, studying God's word and teaching it to others, working to acquire the fruit of the spirit, and all other commandments which promote spiritual growth. These are the things which constitute the *summum bonum,* the highest good, the best of life.

We must strive constantly to keep our sense of values straight, for it is so easy to get caught up into the whirl of daily activities and to fail to give emphasis to those things "which shall not be taken away." Surely the Lord is grieved as he looks upon the world today and sees so many people scurrying around, spending their lives on that which goes bankrupt at the grave.

III. THE SUPERIORITY OF SPIRITUAL VALUES.

Many other Scriptures teach the relative importance of spiritual and material values.

"A man's life consisteth not in the abundance of things which he possesseth" (Lk. 12:15). Real living is not made of "things," though possessions are necessary and not wrong within themselves. The person whose life is centered around "the good part, which shall not be taken away," can enjoy making a living, keeping a house, rest, recreation and fellowship with others — for he understands that these are the mere fringes of life. They are good, but merely the stage, the drapery and the setting for real living. The person who centers his life around these alone and neglects the spiritual is like one who builds an elaborate stage equipped with the finest settings and waits for a play which never shows.

"For what shall it profit a man, if he shall gain the whole world, and lose his own soul?" (Mk. 8:36). One soul is worth more than all the world. One can become so engrossed in working toward prosperity that he tends to measure all attainment in terms of the material and to feel that he is a real success if he has acquired the comforts and luxuries of this world. This attitude can completely stifle one's spiritual nature.

> Have you only comfort, and the lust for comfort, that stealthy thing that enters the house a guest, and then becomes a host, and then a master? Though its hands are silken, its heart is of iron. The lust for comfort murders the passions of the soul and then walks grinning at the funeral.

This is what happened to the rich fool who became enamored with his own success and so engrossed with his barns and his goods that his soul starved to death (Lk. 12:19-21). He was called a fool because "he layeth up treasure for himself, and is not rich toward God."

"Labor not for the meat that perisheth, *but for that meat which endureth unto everlasting life*" (Jno. 6:27). Does this mean that it is wrong to work for food? Of course not, for we have already studied that this is God's will. Therefore, this verse is showing the relative insignificance of physical food when compared with spiritual food.

"Lay not up for yourselves treasures upon earth . . . *but lay up for yourselves treasures in heaven*" (Matt. 6:19,20). Does this teach that it is wrong to save money? No, for we have already studied Scriptures which show the wisdom of such. Therefore, this verse shows the superiority of spiritual or heavenly treasures when compared with earthly treasures. We must never lose sight of this distinction.

"And fear not them which kill the body, but are not able to kill the soul: *but rather fear him which is able to destroy both soul and body in hell*" (Matt. 10:28). The soul is so much more important than the body, for one is temporal and the other is eternal.

The ministry of the Word is superior to serving tables (Acts 6:1-4). Again we see that all things concerning the welfare of the soul should take precedence over that which involves the body. Preaching the gospel is the primary work of the church and so much more important than feeding and clothing the needy.

Spiritual attainment is more valuable than costly jewels: (1) To possess godly wisdom is more precious than rubies (Prov. 3:15; 8:11). (2) "That the trial of your faith, being much more precious than of gold that perisheth, though it be tried with fire" (I Pet. 1:7). How could the trial of our faith be more precious than gold? It is a treasure which helps toward spiritual growth, and this is more valuable than the gold that perishes. (3) The woman who is virtuous and worthy according to God's standards is worth more than costly treasures, "for her price is far above rubies" (Prov. 31:10).

"But seek ye first the kingdom of God, and his righteousness; and all these things shall be added unto you" (Matt. 6:33).

IV. THE GOOD AND THE EVIL ATTACHED TO THIS WORLD.

"Love not the world, neither the things that are in the world" (I Jno. 2:15). Since God has enjoined many earthly responsibilities upon us, then what is to be avoided? We should keep in mind that the "world" is used by God in three different senses:

(1) "The world" — meaning the people of the world: "For God so loved the world" (Jno. 3:16). We, too, are to love the world in this sense.

(2) "The world" — meaning the physical universe: "I pray not that thou shouldst take them out of the world" (Jno. 17:15). This universe was made to supply man's needs and is therefore good, but temporary.

(3) "The world" — meaning all things, people and influences which are contrary to the spiritual law of God, opposed to right. These are the things which are sinful, as stated in I John 2:16: "For all that is in the world, the lust of the flesh, and the lust of the eyes, and the pride of life, is not of the Father, but is of the world."

Therefore, we can ask ourselves these questions concerning all things in this world:

(1) Is it evil? Does it violate any part of God's law?

(2) Is it good, but temporary? Is it within God's law, and yet a part of those things which we merely use here for awhile?

(3) Is it good and eternal? Will it promote the welfare of the soul and build up those values "which shall not be taken away" from us?

REVIEW EXERCISE

1. "Whatsoever ye do in _____ or _____, do all in the name of the Lord."

2. What does it mean to do something in the name of the Lord?
_____

3. Name some material works which have been commanded by God.
_____

4. The physical deeds of the good Samaritan were evidence of a spiritual quality, _____.

5. What does God say of the man who refuses to support his family?
_____

6. What does God say of the woman who neglects her responsibilities? _____

7. What is "the good part" of life? _____

8. What did Mary do to show her supreme devotion to Christ? ____

_____

9. In what three senses does God use the word "world"? ____
_____
_____

10. "Present your bodies a _____ _____."

11. (T or F) John 6:27 teaches that it is wrong to work.

12. (T or F) Matthew 6:19,20 teaches that it is wrong to save.

13. Name some things which are more valuable than costly jewels.

FOR THOUGHT OR DISCUSSION

1. Discuss the inspiring example of Job who held tenaciously to eternal values in the midst of hardships on every side. Though he was stripped of material possessions, his life had been built upon "that which shall not be taken away."

2. Think of all the things Mary could have done with her precious ointment, or with the money for which it could have been sold. Are we willing to give our best to the Master?

9.

"Troubled About Many Things"

"**M**ARTHA, Martha, thou art careful and troubled about many things" (Lk. 10:41). So spoke Christ. Martha was filled with care and trouble. Why? Over nothing more than the preparation of a meal. From the proverbial molehill she had created a mountain, and over it she fretted and stewed to such an extent that it caused her to act in an unbecoming way. Christ gently chided to help her regain her sense of values.

All of us can sympathize with Martha, for we live in a fast-moving age in which so many things can cause tenseness and anxiety. We can also profit much from Christ's words to her. Ours has been called the "age of the aspirin." Our world is filled with problems both real and imaginary, ranging all the way from petty annoyances to heartbreaking tragedies, so that it is easy for the heart to be enveloped with anxiety. One character in an American novel says: "I feel like I have enough chaos in me for the Lord to make another world out of." He merely expressed what so many feel.

Many doctors have labeled worry as Public Enemy Number One. The prevalence and seriousness of this problem is established by the fact that of all hospital beds in our nation, one half is filled with patients suffering from some degree of mental distress, and an estimated one-fourth of all medical prescriptions is for some type of tranquilizer. To adjust to the constant stress is a daily challenge. Within ourselves we have no knowledge, but in the remainder of this book we shall simply glean some solutions from God's word. This cannot be done in one chapter, and thus the next five chapters should be studied as a unit.

I. "TAKE NO THOUGHT."

Anxiety is our problem, but it has always been so. Christ not only taught Martha concerning it, but in the Sermon on the Mount he said: "Take no thought for your life, what ye shall eat, or what ye shall drink; nor yet for your body, what ye shall put on" (Matt. 6:25). The Holy Spirit also said: "In nothing be anxious" (Phil. 4:6, A.S.V.).

In determining Christ's meaning, consider some things he is not teaching: He is not advocating indolence in providing for family (I Tim. 5:8). He does not mean for us to be unconcerned over the state of our fellowman (Matt. 25:32-46). He does not teach indifference toward the souls of others (Lk. 19:41). He is not advising slothfulness in keeping a house (Tit. 2:5) or in rearing a family (Eph. 6:4). He is not teaching us to be unconcerned over the welfare of the church (II Cor. 11:28).

Some who have accomplished much have been at some time in their lives chronic worriers. This is because they were sensitive, discerning people who cared enough to sense the world's needs and to labor toward a solution. They had to learn to control this tendency, to harness this concern.

When Charles H. Spurgeon first began preaching, he worried about his sermons — even to the extent of hoping he would break a leg before time to preach. Then one day he asked himself: "What is the worst thing that can happen to me during my sermon?" Whatever it might be, he decided that it would not be a world-shaking disaster. When he looked at his problem in its true perspective, he relaxed and became a very outstanding speaker of his generation. A tendency to worry can be a quality of strength instead of weakness, but only after it is conquered and channeled into constructiveness rather than destructiveness.

Christ is teaching against being over-anxious. What is anxiety? Webster defines it: "A condition of mental uneasiness arising from fear or distress, especially concerning possible misfortune or some uncertain future event."

II. SAND IN OUR SHOES.

Just for the novelty of it a man walked from California to New York. An interviewer asked him to tell the greatest difficulty he had encountered, expecting him to mention some hazardous mountain or turbulent river or burning desert. But not so. The man replied: "It was the sand in my shoes." How true of life. Many times we can surmount the gravest obstacles, only to fall victim to the comparatively trivial things which plague us day by day.

There is another difference. The mountains and rivers and deserts cannot be changed; we adjust ourselves to them — but sand in the shoes can be controlled. It can be emptied from the shoes; and if more accumulates, it can be emptied again.

In this lesson we will consider some of the common causes of anxiety which can be changed or removed. There are mountains which cannot be moved, deserts which cannot be cooled, and the surmounting of these obstacles will be discussed in the following chapter.

III. BEING OVERCOME WITH CARES OF THE WORLD.

A well-known doctor observed that three very common things tend to promote daily anxiety: the clock, the telephone, and the calendar. The clock symbolizes the pressure of constant deadlines we must meet. The telephone is indicative of frequent interruptions; and the calendar is a continual reminder of the uncertainties of the future. This is indeed an apt commentary on our time.

Martha was simply overcome with the hustle and bustle of everyday living. Preparing a meal was not evil, but it was just so close to her eyes that it obscured her vision of more important things. You know, we can take a very small object and hold it so close to our eyes that we can see nothing else. This is what Martha had done. At the time, she thought she had a big problem. Did she? She had built a simple duty into a monumental task and a trivial annoyance into a mountain of self-pity. Later in her life she faced real trials and heartaches when death entered her home — and surely at that time she could look backward and realize how foolish she had been to place so much emphasis on the cares of the world. This is one thing which produces nervousness and frustration.

IV. PUTTING TOO MUCH EMPHASIS ON MATERIAL THINGS.

"A man's life consisteth not in the abundance of things which he possesseth" (Lk. 12:15). One who considers the accumulation of possessions the criterion of success feels a constant sense of frustration, for he can always look at the material ladder and see someone a little higher up. The person who fully realizes that real living is dependent upon what he has within him rather than without him can relax and enjoy what he has and work toward attainment of that "which shall not be taken away."

When you become tense and anxious about many things, ask yourself: Is it merely an over-emphasis of material things?

V. SELF-PITY.

This is a common enemy of the peaceful mind. It saps energy, mars personality and destroys usefulness. This was one of Martha's major problems. As she labored over a hot fire, she felt sorrier and sorrier for herself. Poor me! Finally her self-pity led her to speak sharply and unbecomingly to Christ who was a guest in her home. In effect she said: "You don't even care what happens to me. Why don't you tell Mary to help me?"

With a different outlook Martha could have changed the atmosphere of the whole day for herself, for Mary and for Christ. Less selfishness would have led her to be grateful for the privilege of cooking for the Master. She could have been so glad that Mary was hearing the Lord's words — but she wasn't thinking of Mary's welfare; she could think only of herself.

There is but one cure for self-pity, and that is to center the thoughts outside of oneself and to become thoughtful and involved in the welfare of others (Phil 2:3,4).

VI. CAN ANXIETY ADD ONE CUBIT?

Jesus said: "Which of you by taking thought can add one cubit unto his stature?" (Matt. 6:27). Will all the worry in the world make you grow taller? Of course not, and how foolish to try it. Yet we oftentimes do things just as foolish. How? By fretting over many things which cannot be changed. Some have almost ruined their lives by brooding over the fact that they were not born taller or shorter or some way different. Contentment can come only through acceptance of ourselves as we are, and even people born with severe physical handicaps have lived rich and radiant lives. Think of such people as Helen Keller, Fanny J. Crosby and many others.

The past is another thing which cannot be changed. Think for a moment. Can any amount of despondency cause even the slightest event of the past to "unhappen"? Of course not. Nothing is as unalterable as the past. The art of living must include the art of leaving, of leaving the past which cannot be changed and pressing on to the opportunities of the future. One can be forgiven of past mistakes, but all the tears in the world will not wash away the deed. This has been forcibly expressed by Omar Khayyam:

> The Moving Finger writes, and having writ
> Moves on; nor all your piety nor wit
> Shall lure it back to cancel half a line
> Nor all thy tears wash out a word of it.

VII. "KEEP YOUR EYE ON THE DOUGHNUT."

A clinical psychologist, Dr. Murray Banks, does much counseling and lecturing on good mental attitudes, for this is a problem faced by every person. He concludes one of his lectures by saying that if he were to sum up his advice on how to have the proper and healthful outlook each day it would be this: "Keep your eye on the doughnut instead of the hole." This is simply to say: look at what we have instead of what we lack. Dr. Banks did not originate this principle. It came from God.

We can either look at what we have and count ourselves rich, or look at what we lack and make ourselves poor. We can think constantly of what we lack and be continually unhappy, for this is a never-fail formula for misery. Or we can think constantly of what we have and be happy and grateful, for gratitude is one of the greatest of all gloom-chasers. How often we fail to count our blessings.

Examine yourself. At which do you spend the most time: thinking of the things you have and being grateful for them? or thinking of the things you lack and being discontented? "Keep your eye on the doughnut instead of the hole," and your day can be filled with joy and contentment. The ability to do this was expressed by the poet, John Kendrick Bangs:

If there's no sun I still can have the moon,
And if there's no moon the stars my need suffice.
Or if these fail I have my evening lamp,
Or — lampless — there's my trusty tallow dip.
And if the dip goes out, my couch remains
Where I may sleep and dream there's light again!

VIII. FEAR CAUSES MUCH ANXIETY.

Fear of the future. A survey to determine what people worried about most indicated that 30% of all worries concerned things in the past which cannot be changed, and 40% involved things which people feared would happen in the future, most of which never happened. Some who heroically bear today's heartaches fear that tomorrow's will be heavier than they can stand. The best cure for this is living a day at a time, as discussed in the next chaper. As the doctor said, the calendar is a daily reminder of the uncertainty of the future; but this anxiety can be controlled by faith in God's promises.

Some of your hurts you have cured,
And the sharpest you still have survived,
But what torments of grief you endured
From the evils which never arrived.
—Emerson

Fear of society, of what people may think, say or do. "The Lord is my helper, and I will not fear what man shall do unto me" (Heb. 13:6).

Fear of losing loved ones. Can anxiety prevent the anticipated loss?

Fear of death. Though we know death is coming, some fear it to the extent of the late William Randolph Hurst who reportedly prohibited the mention of the word in his presence. This is folly, for it did not prevent his death. To face its reality and prepare for it is the only answer, and we can do so without fear. "Yea, though I walk through the valley of the shadow of death, I will fear no evil" (Psa. 23:4). We are born to die. "He who fears death has missed the point of life" — John Erskine. This does not produce a morbid existence. Quite the contrary, it adds zest to living. A Latin poet expressed it in this manner:

> Death plucks me by the ear and says,
> "Live — I am coming."

IX. SINS OF THE HEART.

Some very common causes of frustration and anxiety are sins of the heart.

Hatred, if allowed to bloom in the heart, can shatter one's nerves and bring him to a point of complete breakdown. The cost of "getting even" is too high for any person to pay. It is so easy to see why God has forbidden it, because it will destroy peace of mind and produce nothing but fretful and distressing hours. Hate sometimes harms the hated, but always harms many times more the hate-filled soul. It is so terrible that God calls it murder (I Jno. 3:15).

Envy is another boomerang which comes back to its possessor with greater force. It will eat away the bigness of the soul, for it is a canker, the "rottenness of the bones" (Prov. 14:30). Nothing will make you bluer than being green with envy. What is envy? It is a feeling of distress or unhappiness over the good fortune of others. One prone to envy goes through life doubly miserable, for he is pained not only by his own failures but also by the successes of others. Many otherwise good people do not realize that envy is a grievous sin which can destroy the soul (Gal. 5:21).

Pride can also produce many anxious hours, for it will cause us to be too concerned about what we have or don't have, what other people think about us. It is not wrong to want the favor of our fellowman, for even Christ possessed this to a certain extent (Lk. 2:52). However, it can become sinful if we allow the opinions of others to control our lives and fill us with the fear we may not be constantly elevated in their sight.

REVIEW EXERCISE

1. What are some of the things about which God wants us to be concerned? _____

_____

_____

2. Define anxiety: _____

_____

3. What reason does Hebrews 13:6 give for not being fearful?_____

_____

4. How serious is the sin of hatred in God's sight? _____

   Scripture: _____

5. How does God describe envy? _____

   Scripture: _____

6. Give the four-fold growth of Christ as stated in Luke 2:52_____

_____

_____

7. (T or F) The "abundance of things" will make an abundant life.

8. (T or F) Worry can "add one cubit" to your stature.

9. "I will fear no evil, for _____"

   Scripture: _____

FOR THOUGHT OR DISCUSSION

1. How do you think it would have affected the apostle Paul's life if he had spent much time in brooding over his past mistakes? Rather, what was his attitude?

2. Suppose Joseph had spent his days in bitterness, brooding over the

past and his brothers' mistreatment of him. Do you think he could have accomplished what he did?

3. Discuss. some practical things to do if you begin to have a feeling of self-pity.

4. Discuss this summary of reasons for not being over-anxious:

(1) Our anxiety will not change anything in the past.

(2) Worry will not ward off an anticipated evil. "Worry never robs tomorrow of its sorrow; it only robs today of its strength."

(3) What seems to be evil may turn out for good (Rom. 8:28).

(4) Anxiety is a disregard of a divine command.

(5) It shows distrust in the promises of God.

(6) Anxiety keeps us from doing the things we should do today.

(7) It can be very harmful to our health.

10.

The Power of His Presence

WHEN the wise old Roman scholar, Antonious Praeus, was on his death-bed, he was asked what he considered the most valuable quality for a person to master. Thoughtfully he replied: "Equanimity." That is, the ability to adjust to circumstances and to keep one's balance in spite of difficulties. No matter how successfully we live the Christian life and master the problems of daily stresses, there will be times of intense heartache and discouragement produced by circumstances completely beyond our control. This was true of the godly Job, who said: "Man that is born of woman is of few days and full of trouble" (Job 14:1). No condition of life is so certain, so universal and so acute as the troubled heart. Such a time came in the lives of Mary and Martha, and these times will come to us.

I. WE MUST EXPECT ADVERSITY WHICH IS BEYOND OUR CONTROL.

Understanding that these crises are inevitable, we should strive beforehand to build the strength and faith necessary to sustain us. In our last chapter we discussed some things we can change. Now let's think of some things we cannot change. In such cases, we have only two alternatives. We can either accept the circumstances and adjust our own thinking and reactions to them; or we can destroy ourselves by resisting that which cannot be changed.

Loss of loved ones. This is a heartache which comes in time to every person. The only possible comfort must come from the promises of Christ, as we shall witness in the bereavement of Mary and Martha.

Sickness, either of our own or our loved ones. These bodies were not made for an eternal existence, and in time they will weaken and perish.

Persecution or mistreatment by others. This was experienced by all the great men of God such as Joseph, Elijah, Stephen, Paul and Christ. The servant is not above his Master, and "All that will live godly in Christ Jesus shall suffer persecution" (II Tim. 3:12). We cannot control the actions of others; we can control only our own reactions to them.

Disappointment in friends and loved ones. Think of the heaviness of heart which must have been David's when his own son Absalom led a rebellious army against his father (II Sam. 15:4; 17:1-14). Death itself brings no keener heartache than this. Yet we cannot control the actions of others; we can control only our own reactions to them.

Criticism is another thing beyond our control. It will come; so it is better to suffer doing right than wrong (I Pet. 3:17). Anyone who accomplishes anything will become the critics' target, and this can cause many frustrating and heartbreaking hours. It has caused capable people to give up in discouragement and to bury their talents. Christ was criticized, vilified and falsely accused, even though he was sinless and did nothing to merit it. We can expect no less. Abraham Lincoln's critics belittled his education, scoffed at his rustic ways, and publicly ridiculed his looks; but he ignored their sneers and forged ahead with the tasks he considered important. Today you remember Lincoln, but can you recall the name of even one of his critics? Again: we cannot con-

trol the actions of others; we can control only our own reactions to them.

> As the bird trims her to the gale,
> I trim myself to the storm of time.
> — Emerson

II. THE FIRST STEP.

In striving to calm the troubled heart, the first step is to
decide whether or not we can remedy the cause of the heartache. If so, we can determine to master the problem, as discussed in the previous chapter. If not, what can help us to
adjust ourselves to uncontrollable circumstances?

III. "LET NOT YOUR HEART BE TROUBLED."

The disciples were troubled because Jesus told them that
he was soon to leave them. Sensing their shock and dismay,
he said: "Let not your heart be troubled" (Jno. 14:1). This
consoling and tender admonition furnished for them and for
us one of the most needed of all teachings. No Scripture por-
trays more beautifully the complete humanity and also the
complete deity of Jesus. Because he had lived in the flesh
and experienced the troubled heart, he could sympathetically
understand their anxiety. On the other hand, because he was
divine, he could give them assurances and comfort which no
man could give.

"Let not your heart be troubled." Why? "Ye believe in
God, believe also in me . . . I go to prepare a place for you."
Faith and hope — Jesus specifies the two most necessary balms
for the troubled heart. Faith in a power greater than man
and a hope of something better than this world dispel our fears
and quieten our hearts. The only hope of humanity must
be vertical, for we are beyond a horizontal reach. Unless we
reach up, we travel like men walking in quicksand. Jeremiah
arose from his weeping to remind men that they should not
glory in wisdom, nor might, nor riches, but in an understand-

ing of God's power (Jer. 9:23,24). This is the only solution, and the person who does not possess faith and hope must
live and die with a trouble-racked spirit.

These two necessary ingredients for weathering life's
storms are seen in the lives of Mary and Martha. "Now a
certain man was sick, named Lazarus, of Bethany, the town
of Mary and her sister Martha . . . Therefore his sisters sent
unto him saying, Lord, behold, he whom thou lovest is sick"
(Jno. 11:1-3). But Jesus did not arrive in time, and Lazarus
died. Mary and Martha wept openly and grieved deeply. As
Jesus approached Bethany, Martha hurried to the edge of the
village to meet him and said: "Lord, if thou hadst been here,
my brother had not died." When Mary heard that Jesus had
come, she hastened to meet him and she, too, said: "Lord, if
thou hadst been here, my brother had not died." These words
indicate the supreme faith they had in Jesus, in his power and
his deity. They had not only faith but also a strong hope:
"Martha said unto him, I know that he shall rise again in the
resurrection at the last day." This was prior to Lazarus' resurrection by Jesus, and even then Martha had a sure hope
of life beyond the grave. Then Christ first made to Martha
the pronouncement which produced hope and consolation for
her and for all humanity from that time until now: "I am the
resurrection, and the life: he that believeth in me, though he
were dead, yet shall he live" (Jno. 11:25).

Jesus raised Lazarus from the dead, not for the benefit of
Lazarus, for it was no blessing to him to return to this realm of
sickness and sorrow; but it was to produce faith and hope in
the human heart. It confirmed then and now the reality of
a future life and God's power to raise us from the dead. It
gives us hope of seeing our loved ones beyond the grave. It
is indeed sorrowful and desolate either to live without hope or to
see loved ones live and die without hope (I Thess. 4:13).

IV. "NEITHER LET IT BE AFRAID."

Jesus said to the apostles: "Let not your heart be troubled, neither let it be afraid" (Jno. 14:27). The troubled heart is so often filled with fear. To feel fear is no sign of weakness, for as Emerson expressed it: "He has not learned the lesson of life who does not every day surmount a fear." Our strength comes from conquering our fears, not in refusing to admit their existence.

Fear can be conquered, as mentioned in the previous chapter, but only by faith in God and his promises. Nothing else is strong enough to subdue it.

V. "FOR OUR PROFIT."

"*For whom the Lord loveth he chasteneth,* and scourgeth every son whom he receiveth" (Heb. 12:6). Why? ". . . for our profit, that we might be partakers of his holiness" (Heb. 12:10). The major purpose of life is not comfort but holiness, that our inner beings may be molded into a God-likeness fit to spend eternity with him. This cannot be achieved in the sunlight; it must be formed in the shadows, for adversity is to the spirit what exercise is to the body. Without it, there can be no maturity. Our natural tendency is to shrink back from hardships and to count them as curses; but we should welcome them as blessings which provide the means of spiritual growth. Weary and battle-scarred soldiers of the cross' can look backward on their lives and know that this is true.

George Matheson, blind preacher of Scotland, said:

My God, I have never thanked thee for my thorn. I have thanked thee a thousand times for my roses, but not once for my thorn. I have been looking forward to a world where I shall get compensation for my cross; but I have never thought of my cross as itself a present glory.

Teach me the glory of my cross; teach me the value of my thorn. Show me that I have climbed to thee by the path of pain. Show me that my tears have made my rainbows.

Have you ever seen an old harper handling his harp? He loves the instrument and strokes it gently — until the time when it must be tuned. Then he must grasp it firmly and strike a cord with a quick and harsh blow. If the note is false, he must strain the string until it sometimes is ready to snap with tension before the true note is achieved. So it is with God. Loving us, he sees that which is out of tune and must chasten us perhaps again and again until our rebellious wills give way and in humble submission cry: "Not my will but thine be done."

Great lives testify that adversity increases strength. When David was hiding in caves to preserve his life against the murderously envious Saul, he produced some of the greatest psalms. As Christ faced Gethsemane, he gave some soul-stirring and comfort-producing words which have blessed mankind through all ages. This is true even in secular fields. Luther Burbank was a semi-invalid working in a hot dusty plant. Ill health forced him to quit his work. He later went to California and began working with plants outdoors in the sunshine. As a result, he became one of the world's leading naturalists. With better health, it may be that he never would have accomplished anything worthy of note.

The ancient Phrygians had a legend that every time they conquered an enemy, they absorbed the strength of the vanquished and added it to their own strength. It is true that every time we conquer a temptation or a trial we are made stronger and more able to bear even heavier burdens.

Wherever the light is brightest, there the shadows are the darkest. Let's remember that the converse is also true: wherever the shadows are darkest, the light is shining the brightest. Life is a series of light and shadows, hills and valleys. By these experiences men grow. Someone has expressed it like this: "Be like tea; its real strength appears when it gets in hot water."

VI. LIFE IS BUT A DAY AT MOST.

Each day carries all the burdens and heartaches we need. Christ expressed it like this: "Sufficient unto the day is the evil thereof" (Matt. 6:34). This moment is all we have; life is but a day at most. Yet so many of us crucify today between two thieves: yesterday and tomorrow, thieves because we allow them to steal from us the joys and opportunities of today. Some live each day in memory of a happier yesterday and count themselves unhappy today, while others consume themselves each day with regrets over past mistakes. Others spend each day with the intentions of tomorrow, overlooking the opportunities of today. The great word in the Bible is today (Heb. 3:13).

Dr. Osler observed: "The freshest, the oldest, the usefulest of all rules for mental health is to live cne day at a time." We should receive profit from past mistakes, strength from comforting memories and encouragement from future plans — all the time keeping in mind that today is all we have. Living today to the fullest is the best preparation for tomorrow and the best way to have happy memories of yesterday.

> Build a little fence of trust
>   Around today;
> Fill the space with loving deeds,
>   And therein stay,
> Look not through the sheltering bars
>   Upon tomorrow;
> God will help thee bear what comes
>   Of joy or sorrow.
>   — Mary Frances Butts

VII. "HE THAT LOSETH HIS LIFE."

Christ said: "He that loseth his life for my sake shall find it" (Matt. 10:39). This is one of the glorious paradoxes of

Christianity. Submerging ourselves in something greater than ourselves, we find the life we desire. We can soothe the sorrowful heart by laying it upon the altar of self-forgetfulness and service to God and fellowman.

Before the first World War there was a lady who had moved many years previously to a small New England community. She grieved her heart out through the years because she was never accepted into the town's socially elite circles. She decided to travel to Europe, hoping that upon her return she would be accepted into the town's Literary Society, which she had long desired. She was in Europe when the war broke out and was unable to return home. She volunteered as a nurse and spent several months helping the wounded in one of the hospitals. When she arrived home, one of her friends said to her: "Now perhaps you will be elected to the Literary Society." The lady calmly and thoughtfully replied: "You know, it doesn't matter to me any more whether I am a member or not." She had submerged herself in useful service and found the contentment so long coveted.

No wonder a part of God's formula for happiness is: "But he that is greatest among you shall be your servant" (Matt. 23:11). This is one of the avenues to the quiet and peaceful heart.

VIII. THOUGHT CAN FORM AN INNER CORE OF QUIETUDE.

Whether our distress is minor or major, its conquest must be won within the mind. When we find ourselves troubled about many things we should think on the God-given principles just discussed. We can develop within ourselves an inner core of quietude. Christ was able to do this. Imagine yourself in a place of cool and peaceful quiet, surrounded by a high protective wall through which no dangerous or threatening force may pass. You can sit there in a place of peace, though all the trouble of the world may beat upon that wall. Think of the word tranquility. Does it not have a soothing sound? Think of the word serenity. Does it not contain comfort? And with thoughts of faith, hope, gratitude, optimism and determination we can build our own sanctuary of quietude within our spirits, though in the midst of disquietude all around.

It helps to remember that no outside force in the world is powerful enough to cause us to lose our souls. This is the teaching of Romans 8:35-39. We can become estranged from God, because the Bible tells of some who did; but such separation comes from within the heart of man. Understanding this helps to bear tribulation and discouragement.

Martha said: "Lord, if thou hadst been here." She had faith in Christ's ability to handle every distress. The Lord is here to help us, and he is still able to handle every adversity. "Lo I am with you alway, even unto the end of the world." "Draw nigh unto God, and he will draw nigh unto you." "The Lord is my helper; I will not fear what man can do unto me."

REVIEW EXERCISE

1. How did Job describe man's life? ....

2. What heartache did Absalom bring upon his father? ....

....

3. What does I Peter 3:17 teach about suffering hardships? ....

....

4. Name some of the unchangeable circumstances which often envelop mankind. ....

....

....

5. What is the first step we should take in an effort to conquer our problems? ....

....

6. What are the two most important things necessary to soothe the troubled heart? ....

.... - ....

7. Why does the Lord chasten those he loves? ....

8. "He that loseth his life .... shall find it."

9. What ingredient of greatness does Christ give in Matthew 23:11?

....

10. What two great "I ams" did Christ say to Martha? ....

....

11. (T or F) No force outside ourselves can cause us to lose our souls.

12. Jeremiah admonished men not to glory in ....

but in ....,

FOR THOUGHT OR DISCUSSION

1. Look backward on your life and think how various hardships have served to promote spiritual growth, to bring you closer to the Lord.

2. When you think of the despair in the heart of those who live without hope of life beyond the grave, doesn't it encourage you to serve God more willingly and sacrificially?

11.

"My Peace I Give Unto You"

ONE of the keenest longings of the heart is for peace within. To the trouble-hearted apostles Jesus said: "Peace I leave with you: my peace I give unto you" (Jno. 14:27). Surely he wants all his followers to share in this bequest, but how can it be done? Is it sufficient simply for Christ to say: "My peace I give unto you"? No. Christ has already done his part. By word and example he furnished the pattern for a peaceful heart. It has been summed up by the Holy Spirit: "To be spiritually minded is life and peace" (Rom. 8:6). Life and peace! But the attainment is conditional: "to be spiritually minded." What does this involve?

I. ONE MUST DESIRE TO BE A SPIRITUAL PERSON.

"To be spiritually minded is life and peace," but many people have no desire to develop a spiritual mind. They go through life wondering why they have never attained the peaceful heart, all the time ignoring God's formula for acquiring it. We must learn to love spiritual things here. If not, we will not be fit for heaven, and would be miserable there even if the Lord should allow us to go.

The first step is for one to become a Christian and to determine to walk in the ways of God.

II. SPIRITUALITY AND PEACE MUST BEGIN IN THE MIND.

"Be not conformed to this world: but be ye transformed by the renewing of your mind" (Rom. 12:2). This is in complete harmony with the above Scripture: "For to be carnally minded is death; but to be spiritually minded is life and peace"

(Rom. 8:6). The transformation must begin by renewing the mind. How can this be done? The mind is never a vacuum. For example, suppose that I should tell you not to think of a red hat. What are you thinking about right now? A red hat, of course. It does little good to tell ourselves: "I am not going to think about this or that." This only causes the mind to dwell on the very thing we are striving to drive from the mind. Rather, we must fill the mind with other thoughts, good thoughts, and there will be no room for thoughts of fear, frustration, discouragement, hatred or bitterness.

It is impossible to think carnal thoughts and develop into a spiritual person, for "as he thinketh in his heart, so is he" (Prov. 23:7). In God's formula for a beautiful life he has specified the beautiful qualities upon which we should think (Phil. 4:8).

> One cannot think carnality and live spiritually.
> One cannot think fear and act courageously.
> One cannot think courage and act fearfully.
> One cannot think hatred and act lovely.
> One cannot think bitterness and act sweetly.
> One cannot think sweetness and act bitterly.
> One cannot think defeat and act victoriously.

Happiness is a state of mind which must be produced within our own thinking or not at all. It is therefore not dependent upon what is around us, but upon what is within us. William Henry Channing was chaplain of the House of Representatives in the middle of the last century. He gave his definition of happiness. Read it and notice how many things must begin with an attitude of mind:

> To live content with small means; to seek elegance rather than luxury, and refinement rather than fashion; to be worthy, not respectable, and wealthy, not rich; to study hard,

think quietly, talk gently, act frankly; to listen to the stars and birds, to babes and sages, with open heart; to bear all cheerfully, do all bravely, await occasions, hurry never; in a word to let the spiritual, unbidden and unconscious, grow up through the common.

An article appeared in the New York Times several years ago on the art of happiness. It was not written by a preacher, but notice how the principles are direct teachings of God. Among other things the writer said:

> There was never a time when so much official effort was being expended to produce happiness, and probably never a time when so little attention was paid by the individual to creating the personal qualities which make for it. What one misses most today is the evidence of widespread personal determination to develop a character that will in itself, given any reasonable odds, make for happiness. Our whole emphasis is on the reform of living conditions, of increased wages, of controls on the economic structure — the government approach — and so little on man improving himself.

> The ingredients of happiness are so simple that they can be counted on one hand. Happiness comes from within, and rests most securely on simple goodness and clear conscience . . . no one is known to have gained it without a philosophy resting on ethical principles. Selfishness is its enemy; to make another happy is to be happy one's self. It is quiet, seldom found for long crowds, most easily won in moments of solitude and reflection. It cannot be bought; indeed money has very little to do with it.

> No one is happy unless he is reasonably well satisfied with himself, so that the quest for tranquility must of necessity begin with self-examination. We shall not often be content with what we discover in this scrutiny. There is so much to do, and so little done. Upon this searching self-analysis, however, depends the discovery of those qualities that make each man unique, and whose development alone can bring satisfaction.

III. "WHAT HAVE THEY SEEN IN THINE HOUSE?" (II Ki. 20:15).

Our thinking is controlled to a large extent by what we see and hear. On the other hand, what we see and hear is indicative of what we enjoy putting into the mind. This being true, when one walks into our home and looks at the books, magazines, records and television programs, he is furnished one index to our mind and the things we enjoy putting into it.

"To be carnally minded is death." It is impossible to be a spiritual person if one feasts the mind on carnal things. "What have they seen in thine house?" Go through your house and make a survey. Check the books, magazines, records and make a list of frequently seen television programs. Will they build up the mind and promote spirituality, or will they tear down and promote carnality? Let's remember what the Lord has said: "To be spiritually minded is life and peace." We cannot have the life and peace we desire unless we fill our minds with spiritual things.

IV. OUR SPIRITUAL CONDITION WILL BE REVEALED BY OUR LANGUAGE.

"Out of the abundance of the heart the mouth speaketh" (Matt. 12:34). If no spirituality appears in one's speech, it is positive proof that none exists in the heart; and therefore it is impossible for that one to have "life and peace." If we would have the peace which Christ has promised, we must learn to control the heart which will in turn control the tongue. This is such a serious matter, "For by thy words thou shalt be justified, and by thy words thou shalt be condemned" (Matt. 12:37).

What is the language which God forbids? Murmuring and complaining (Phil. 2:14; I Cor. 10:10). Lying (Rev. 21:8). Impure speech (Col. 3:8; Eph. 4:29). Profanity

(Ex. 20:7). Gossip (Lev. 19:16; I Tim. 5:13). Fault-finding (Matt. 7:3-5). Harsh and unkind words (Prov. 31:26). Contention and nagging (Prov. 19:13; 27:15). Meddling (I Thess. 4:11; Prov. 20:3). Hasty words (Eccl. 5:2; Prov. 29:20). Idle words (Matt. 12:36).

There is a story about a fox who attempted to creep under a stone wall to steal grapes. He ran against a wire which set a big bell rattling. He drew back, alarmed, and waited until the bell became silent. He repeated the effort, with the same result. He tried the third time, and when the bell had ceased its clanging, he looked up at it and said:

> A long tongue, and a hollow head;
> A great noise, and nothing said.

V. THE PEACE-BESTOWING POWER OF GRATITUDE.

The spiritual mind is filled with faith and hope, as seen in our previous chapter. These form the basis for the peaceful heart, but there are other qualities of the spirit which ennoble lives and enhance spiritual beauty. One of these is gratitude, which can do so much to enrich each day. We can understand why God has commanded gratitude and has labeled ingratitude as wickedness (Rom. 1:21). Think of things for which we should be daily thankful.

Thankful for life itself. We take our lives for granted and most live as though we will be here forever. Only after one has looked death in the face can he appreciate the gift of life. This is the reason that many soldiers have returned home maimed for life and yet have been filled with gratitude and free of bitterness. As one expressed it: "I am too grateful to be alive. I am one of the lucky ones. So many of my buddies did not come back."

Thankful for health. If you are able to be up today, you are fortunate; and we really do not realize how fortunate we are until the day comes that we cannot get up. Health is so good and wonderful that one of the great wishes of the Bible concerns it (III Jno. 2). Even though you may be ill today, you can think of others who are in worse condition than you are.

Thankful for spiritual blessings. Suppose you lived in a nation where you had never had the privilege of learning of God and Christ.

Thankful for family and friends. With all your problems and heartaches, do you know of anyone with whom you would exchange places today? No, you don't; for then you would have to give up your family and friends. This thought should make us daily grateful.

Thankful for material blessings. Though we are showered with material blessings, too many spend their days thinking on things they do not have. When you are tempted to do this, read the following which was submitted to a newspaper and has been published in a number of periodicals. So many have requested copies of it that we are including it in this series. It is an old Kentucky "receipt" on how Grandma did the washing. It is supposed to be genuine, including the spelling. It was published under the caption: "Grandma Had a Tranquilizer."

1. Bild a fire in back yard to heet kettle of rain water.
2. Set tubs so smoke won't blow in eyes if wind is pert.
3. Shave one hole cake soap in bilin water.
4. Sort things, make three piles, 1 pile white, 1 pile cullord, 1 pile work britches and rags.
5. Stur flour in cold water to smooth, then thin down with bilin water.
6. Rub dirty spots on board, scrub hard, then bile, rub cullord but don't bile — just rench and starch.

7. Take white things out of kettle with broom stick handle, then rench, blew and starch.

8. Spred tee towels on grass.

9. Hang old rags on fence.

10. Pore rench water in flower bed.

11. Scrub porch with hot soapy water.

12. Turn tubs upside down.

13. Go put on clean dress — smooth hair with side combs — brew a cup of tea — set back and rest a spell and count your blessings.

VI. COMMUNICATION LINES BETWEEN YOU AND GOD.

We can never enjoy the life and peace which comes from a spiritual mind unless we keep open the communication lines between ourselves and the Lord.

Do we constantly feel the presence of the Lord? David did. He felt so close to God that he was always aware of his presence, his nearness. "Draw nigh to God, and he will draw nigh to you" (Jas. 4:8). In an effort to bring God closer to us, however, some have gone so far as to advocate that we regard God as a "Buddie" and to talk with him in such a manner. Though we should regard God as a friend, we should always keep in mind that he is a Superior Friend, not a buddie — for that term denotes one our own equal. When our hearts are heavy and we are in need, we want One with superior power to help us, not a buddie. We are not subject to nor accountable to a buddie, but we are to God. We are in no way his equal; and in our effort to feel near the Lord, it is neither necessary nor right to pull him down to our level.

Nothing can equal the strengthening power which comes from a realization that we are on the Lord's side, that he is on ours, that he is concerned about us and ever ready to help us.

The day is long and the day is hard;
We are tired of the march and of keeping guard;
Tired of the sense of a fight to be won,
Of days to live through, and of work to be done;
Tired of ourselves and of being alone.

And all the while, did we only see,
We walk in the Lord's own company;
We fight, but 'tis he who nerves our arm;
He turns the arrows which else might harm,
And out of the storm he brings a calm.
                              — Susan Coolidge

Do we listen to God frequently? We can hear the Lord only by reading his Word (Heb. 1:1,2). Though secular magazines, newspapers and books have a place in our lives, they can never produce the spiritual mind essential for the peaceful heart. If our hearts are filled with unrest, let's ask ourselves: How much have I communicated with God lately through his word?

Do we talk with God often? If we feel his presence at all times, it will be easy to talk with him. Even silently in the midst of people we can direct our hearts to him and talk with him. A mother who was listening to her young son pray commented: "Son, don't bother to give God instructions. Just report for duty." We need to ask him often for guidance. We want the "peace of God with which passeth understanding" — but notice the condition necessary to bring it about: "Be careful for nothing; but in every thing by prayer and supplication with thanksgiving let your requests be made known unto God" (Phil. 4:6,7).

Trouble and perplexity drive us to prayer,
And prayer drives away trouble and perplexity.

REVIEW EXERCISE

1. On what does Philippians 4:8 admonish us to think?........................

----

2. What is the condition upon which we are promised "life and peace"? _____

_____

3. What is the first step toward being transformed? _____

_____

4. "To be carnally minded is _____."

5. (T or F) What we say has nothing to do with our eternal salvation.

    Scripture: _____

6. What does God say about meddling in other people's business?

_____

7. What will be the final state of all liars? _____

    Scripture: _____

8. Who is given as an example to warn us against the sin of murmuring and complaining? _____

9. What was John's wish "unto the well-beloved Gaius"? _____

_____

10. "Draw nigh to God and he will _____"

11. How must improper thoughts be driven from the mind?_____

_____

12. How important are thoughts, as taught in Proverbs 23:7? _____

_____

13. "In everything by _____ and _____

    with_____ let your requests be made known unto God."

FOR THOUGHT OR DISCUSSION

1. Since a clear conscience is one ingredient of happiness, discuss what Paul has to say on this subject in Acts 24:16.

2. Making others happy will also promote our own happiness. In Acts 20:34,35 Paul states that he had not only worked to support himself but also ....

   He concludes with Jesus' words that "it is more blessed to .... than to........................."

3. Your class may want to exchange ideas on books, magazines and periodicals which can help to promote the spiritual growth of yourself and your family.

12.

"And Rest Awhile"

"**A**ND the apostles gathered themselves together unto Jesus, and told him all things, both what they had done, and what they had taught. And he said unto them, Come ye yourselves apart into a desert place, and rest a while: for there were many coming and going, and they had no leisure so much as to eat" (Mk. 6:30,31). The apostles had returned from strenuous missionary travels, and they had gone through the disheartening and sorrowful experience of the beheading of John the Baptist. Thus, Christ called them apart to rest after work, to calm after excitement, to repose after sorrow.

One of our goals is to develop the peaceful heart and to prepare for the eternal rest of the spirit. However, in the text above, Jesus shows also the importance of rest for the physical body.

I. REST WAS ORDAINED BY GOD.

God made the physical bodies to need rest, and has made provision for regular periods of rest. At the giving of the law of Moses, he commanded his people to rest on the seventh day of the week (Ex. 23:12). The annual feasts added other days of rest, as described in Leviticus 23:7,8 and elsewhere. Provisions were made even for periods of rest for the land (Lev. 25:5). A loving Father has commanded both work and rest, because both are essential to man's well-being. The blessings of work have been discussed in a previous chapter. We must also have rest in order to renew both body and spirit and fortify both for future tasks. God knows best and all his laws are given for man's good. William H. Burnham in his

book, *Essentials of Mental Health,* advocates the necessity of
both work and rest: "The fourth condition of mental health
is proper alternation of work and rest. Suitable mental work
is never injurious if it does not last too long and is followed
by adequate rest. A tendency to rhythmic activity is a law of
our nature. The carpenter, the thrasher, the oarsman keep
time in their work. The life of the well man is divided into
alternate periods of labor and rest."

*Man's need and longing for rest are verified by many
Scriptures:*

(1) The blessing of sleep can be most fully appreciated
by those who have experienced the extreme distress of pro-
longed sleeplessness, as Job did: "When I lie down, I say,
When shall I arise, and the night be gone? and I am full of
tossings to and fro unto the dawning of the day" (Job 7:4).

(2) The Psalmist said: "I would fly away and be at rest"
(Psa. 55:6).

(3) Christ experienced weariness of body, and we see him
asleep in the bottom of a ship as a storm raged above him
(Matt. 8:24).

(4) Christ was disappointed that his closest friends had
fallen asleep as he went through the trial of Gethsemane, and
he said to Peter, "What, could ye not watch with me one
hour?" Yet he understood their fatigue and later told them:
"Sleep on now, and take your rest" (Matt. 26:40-45).

(5) Rest is one promise given to the righteous. Of course,
this is primarily rest of spirit, but it also includes physical rest
from work to which we are accustomed in the flesh. "That
they may rest from their labors; and their works do follow
them" (Rev. 14:13). "There remaineth therefore a rest to
the people of God. For he that is entered into his rest, he
also hath ceased from his own works, as God did from his.

Let us labor therefore to enter into that rest, lest any man fall after the same example of unbelief" (Heb. 4:9-11).

II. THE RELATIONSHIP BETWEEN WEARINESS OF BODY AND SPIRIT.

We have considered a number of things which can cause a feeling of frustration and anxiety. Physical fatigue is another factor which should be considered. When we are either ill or tired, the world can look like a mighty dark place and even small tasks can look insurmountably large and difficult. Exhaustion often ushers in dark moods of doubt and fear. When weariness has overtaken us, it is good to remember that the world will not always look so dismal, that oftentimes rest can restore our optimism and brighten our outlook.

This was experienced by Elijah. As he fled from the murderous Jezebel, he went into the wilderness and sat down under a juniper tree. He was so discouraged, so weary of body and spirit, that he wanted to die (I Ki. 19:1-8). He lay down and slept, to be awakened by an angel of God who gave him food: "And he did eat and drink, and laid him down again." After his body had been renewed with rest and food, he was strengthened to continue his work for the Lord.

III. REST THROUGH RELAXATION.

Though sleep is essential, this is not the only means of rest and renewal for the body. It is possible to develop techniques of body relaxation during waking hours which rejuvenate both body and spirit. Thomas A. Edison averaged only four hours of sleep a day during most of his life. However he had the ability to lie down and take a brief nap almost anytime, for he worked relaxed at all times. For this reason, he could fall asleep quickly, rest for a short while and then continue his work.

It has been proved that a person will get along better with

six hours of sleep at night and a brief nap after lunch than
with eight hours of sleep at night and no break during the
day. A friend of ours who carries a tremendously heavy work
load has found this to be true. One of the secrets of his
seemingly boundless energy is the ability to relax completely
at any time. He sleeps ten or fifteen minutes at his office
every afternoon. He awakens refreshed and able to accomplish more during the remainder of the day. He has
also formed another very beneficial habit. When he comes
to a red light as he is driving, he folds his arms and re-
laxes completely until the light changes. This momentarily
relieves his body of all tensions, and as he observed: "I have
learned that the light changes just as fast this way as it does
when I am tense and in a hurry." Someone has commented:
"Some people think they are busy when they are only nervous."
Another has defined nervousness: "Being in a hurry all over."
It is possible for us to be in a hurry all over, caught up in a
frenzy of thought and action, yet not accomplishing anything
at all.

Many times when we become tired, it is not possible for
us to withdraw from the crowds or to go to faraway places
for a vacation. Therefore, we would be wise to develop the
ability of resting both body and spirit even in the midst of
turmoil all around us. This has been thoughtfully expressed
by some unknown poet:

REST WHERE YOU ARE

When, spurred by tasks unceasing or undone,
  You would seek rest afar,
And cannot, though repose be rightly won —
  Rest where you are.

Neglect the needless; sanctify the rest;
  Move without stress or jar;
With quiet of a spirit self-possessed
  Rest where you are.

Not in event, restoration, or release,
  Not in scenes near or far,
But in ourselves are restlessness or peace.
  Rest where you are.

Where lives the soul lives God; his day, his world,
  No phantom mists need mar;
His starry nights are tents of peace unfurled:
  Rest where you are.

IV. REST IN DIVERSION.

Rest for body and spirit is sometimes best found in diversion, not in a cessation of all activity, but in a change of activity. Just as the body requires alternate periods of work and rest, so does the mind. Our Lord understood the importance of relieving the mind from the weighty problems which must be our chief concern of life.

Many men and women laden with burdensome responsibilities have found diversion in sideline activities, and in so doing have not only provided relaxation for themselves but have become notably successful in such fields as painting, music, writing, athletics or horticulture. The more alive a person is the more interest he has in every sphere of human endeavor. David was not only a king. He was also a poet, a musician, a sportsman, a militarist and a philosopher. So was Solomon. The apostle Paul was very well acquainted with poetry and other literature, with the philosophical teachings of his time, with athletics, and with all of the interests and customs of the people with whom he associated. Christ was so conversant with all the spheres of life that he attracted the attention of everyone from the common people to the kings.

The added leisure afforded by modern inventions and techniques has given added opportunities for constructive sideline endeavors which will not only rest our bodies and minds but enrich our lives and benefit others.

Diversion may also be found in social activities. We see Jesus as he attended a marriage feast in Cana of Galilee and participated in the festivities of that joyous occasion (Jno. 2:1-11). The members of the Jerusalem church enjoyed the social life of one another (Acts 2:46). Social activities are a part of the Christian's life, just as they were a part of Christ's life, and they are beneficial and wholesome when kept within the restrictions laid down by God.

Let's consider some tests whereby we can determine whether or not a social activity is good or evil:

(1) The test of dissipation. Many activities which have been labeled recreation are actually dissipation. What is the difference? Recreation is that which re-creates the body and mind, that which rejuvenates and builds up. Dissipation is anything which destroys or tears down. The body is sacred, and condemnation is placed on any person or anything which destroys the body: "What! know ye not that your body is the temple of the Holy Ghost which is in you, which ye have of God, and ye are not your own? For ye are bought with a price: therefore glorify God in your body, and in your spirit, which are God's" (I Cor. 6:19,20).

It is because of their destructive nature that God has forbidden many things. Read the catalog of sins in Galatians 5:19-21 and think on the power which each sin has to destroy either the heart or the body of mankind.

Anything which destroys rather than builds up is a form of dissipation. Even a neighborhood coffee often turns into a destructive social function as women use their tongues to destroy the good name and reputation of others, or to destroy peace in homes and communities by stirring up strife and enlarging differences.

(2) The foresight test. Any activities which may lead to some of the sins listed in Galatians 5:19-21 should be avoided.

It is only smart to consider the end of a road before we start down it. We cannot get to the west coast by traveling east. If some social activity is going in a direction we do not want to travel, it is not smart to engage in it. "A danger sign can't talk, but it is not as dumb as the guy who pays no attention to it."

(3) The test of common sense. A smart person learns from the mistakes of others, but fools never. It is only common sense to recognize what some forms of entertainment have done to others and to avoid them.

(4) The test of one's most admired personality. When we think of engaging in some activity, let's think of the most godly, most admired person we know. Then let's ask ourselves: "Would he or she do this?" If not, then let's forego it; otherwise, we can never grow to be like the one we admire. Of course, at the pinnacle of our admiration is Christ, and it is ideal to ask: "What would Christ do?" Sometimes, however, it helps to consider someone who is wholly human such as we are. Paul could admonish others: "Be ye followers of me, even as I also am of Christ" (I Cor. 11:1).

(5) The test of influence. We must remember that just as we tend to follow others whom we admire, others are being influenced by everything we do. This is true of every person, even though we may think our influence to be small. Christians are to shine as lights in the world (Matt. 5:14-16). If some social function dims our light and influence, then it has not passed the Christian test.

Some activities which are good within themselves may become unwise or wrong because of other things associated with them. For example, swimming is a good and healthful sport, but the immodest dress usually attendant violates a direct command of God (I Tim. 2:9), and dims a Christian's influence, and may lead others to sin.

Several years ago a Christian mother wrote an article: "Live Bait for the Devil's Hook — Furnished by Blinded Mothers." We quote a portion of it:

> Why are little girls kidnapped, shamefully treated and sometimes murdered? In the old days, little girls were taught modesty from infancy, that it was disgraceful to expose the body. Mothers dressed them accordingly. "Old-fashioned," you say? God's word still says, "In like manner also that women adorn themselves in modest apparel."
>
> The devil is the author of many fashions today, and they are inspired by him to destroy the souls of men and women. When God clothed Adam and Eve in the Garden of Eden because they had eaten of the tree of the knowledge of good and evil (Gen. 3), he meant for the human body to be covered from that time on. People who are disregarding this law of God are adding to the crime rampant all over the world today. Mothers, if you go out in public half-naked and allow your innocent little girls to do the same, whose fault is it if they are kidnapped, brutally treated and even murdered? Not the children's fault, for they know no better than they have been taught. God will hold the parents of this generation responsible for not training their children in this aspect of the word of God.

REVIEW EXERCISE

1. What did an angel do for Elijah when he was exhausted and discouraged? ....

2. What social event was attended by Christ? ....

3. "Know ye not that your .... is the temple of the Holy Ghost . . . therefore glorify God in your .... and your ...., which are God's."

4. What sins are specified in Galatians 5:19-21? ....

....

....

5. What is the difference between recreation and dissipation? ....

....

....

6. Quote I Timothy 2:9: ....

....

7. Job suffered many different kinds of distress. Which one is mentioned in this chapter? ....

8. (T or F) Paul wanted people to follow him no matter what he did.

9. What two results of a righteous life are mentioned in Revelation 14:13? ....

....

10. What is one thing which can cause a person to fall from God's favor? ....

(Heb. 4:9-11).

11. To what are Christians compared in Matthew 5:14-16? ....

....

FOR THOUGHT OR DISCUSSION

1. Though the sabbath day, or seventh day of the week, was specified as a day of rest under the law of Moses, the Lord's day, or the first day of the week, is not called a day of rest but is rather designated as a day of worship (Acts 20:7; I Cor. 16:2).

2. Discuss some forms of entertainment which may be right within themselves and yet inexpedient because of things to which they may lead.

13.

Your Alabaster Box

ONE of the most tender and beautiful scenes of Christ's life includes Mary and Martha. During his last troubled days on earth, a supper was given in Bethany at Simon's home. It was a memorable occasion. No doubt the guests talked about the events of that evening long after it had ended. Look at the guest list. There was Lazarus, whom Jesus had so recently raised from the dead, one who had experienced those secrets beyond the mysterious curtain which separates two worlds. His presence testified of our Lord's power over life and death. The Guest of Honor was the very embodiment of life itself — yet One so soon to taste the bitterness of death. Martha — practical, hard-working, faithful, diligent — assisted with the serving. Mary was present — meditative, devoted, grateful. Other disciples, including Judas, were there — men who had shared with Jesus so many triumphs and tribulations of his personal ministry. Knowing that he was soon to face betrayal, a mock trial, and unjust crucifixion, he dined and visited with those he loved so dearly, the inner circle of his closest associates.

As Jesus sat at meat, Mary came "with an alabaster box of ointment of spikenard very precious; and she brake the box, and poured it on his head" (Mk. 14:3). She "anointed the feet of Jesus, and wiped his feet with her hair; and the house was filled with the odor of the ointment" (Jno. 12:3). Judas complained: "Why was not this ointment sold for three hundred pence, and given to the poor?" (Jno. 12:5).

"Then Jesus said, Let her alone: against the day of my

burying hath she kept this" (Jno. 12:7). "She hath done what she could ... Verily I say unto you, Wheresoever the gospel shall be preached throughout the whole world, this also that she hath done shall be spoken of for a memorial of her" (Mk. 14:8,9) — a commendation that has become an everlasting memorial honoring Mary, teaching and encouraging us.

I. A GIFT THAT SPEAKS.

The sacred record does not give one word said by Mary on this occasion, but her gift speaks volumes. Just a little bottle of perfume, but it preaches of motives and attitudes, for from these her actions blossomed.

It preaches of her love for the Master. She loved him wholly, with all her being. Why? For so many reasons:

(1) He was her friend, one with like interests. She was indebted to him for incomparable teachings on the problems of living and dying.

(2) He had raised her beloved brother from the dead and returned him to the family circle.

(3) Jesus loved Mary (Jno. 11:5). It is easy and natural to love those who love us. After the cross, surely she understood more fully the depth of that love.

(4) He was her Lord, the author of her salvation, the hope of her soul, who had made to Martha the pronouncement which has cheered man's heart ever since: "I am the resurrection, and the life: he that believeth in me, though he were dead, yet shall he live" (Jno. 11:25).

Mary's precious gift speaks loudly of her gratitude for all these blessings.

It also tells of a generous heart seeking some means of expressing love and gratitude. One may give without loving, but it is not possible to love without giving. Evidently the costly ointment was the most valuable material possession within her power to bestow. It was a liquid perfume made from highly aromatic nard, or spikenard plants, and imported from the Far East. Historians tell us that the alabaster box was a cruse or long-necked flask made from white spar resembling marble, carved with a delicate beauty to delight the heart of any woman, sealed tightly with wax to preserve the costly perfume. Most likely it was this wax seal which Mary broke, not the entire bottle. The approximate value has been variously estimated. Some have suggested that the average wage-earner's pay was one pence per day (Matt. 20:2). If this should be true, three hundred pence would represent almost a year's wage. In any case, it was so expensive that its profuse use shocked some of the guests. Evidently Mary and Martha were women of wealth and prominence, as this and other considerations have led Bible scholars to conclude.

Mary's gift speaks of humility, and a desire for a personal ministry. Anointing the head of an honored guest was not an uncommon courtesy, but to anoint the feet also was a gesture far beyond the call of duty or hospitality. She did not ask a servant to anoint her Master's feet. As she prostrated herself to dry them with her own hair, she demonstrated that her whole being was subjugated to the will and welfare of Another.

The gift teaches also of courage, for it cost Mary much more than the price of the perfume. It cost the pain and embarrassment of stinging criticism from close friends. We're not surprised by criticism from worldly associates, but real courage is required to withstand rebukes from fellow disciples. But she followed her convictions instead of the crowd. How encouraging it must have been when Jesus threw around her a shield of defense, setting the record straight for everybody then and now.

II. JUDAS' MASK REMOVED.

The history-making evening described in our text is an enlightening study in motives, both good and evil. Mary's perfume became Judas' pitfall. To her it was a stepping-stone; to him, a stumbling-block. The same deed which bared the motives of Mary's heart also exposed the heart of Judas, who said: "Why was not this ointment sold for three hundred pence, and given to the poor?" His vice was masked as a virtue. His feigned concern for the poor was merely a cover for his covetousness. The motive is unmasked for us: "Not that he cared for the poor; but because he was a thief, and had the bag, and bare what was put therein" (Jno. 12:6). Vices are frequently disguised as virtues, and oftentimes the guilty one does not even realize it.

Judas did not give the real reason for his criticism of Mary. People seldom do.

When Judas looked at Mary's gift, all he could see was the dollar mark. His spiritual sight was so darkened that he was blind to the beauty of another's noble deed. Looking through the dollar mark at the expensive perfume, he thought he saw unnecessary extravagance. Some today are so blind to spiritual values that their mental computer quickly sizes up everything in terms of monetary value.

Nothing done for the Lord is wasted. This is one principle Jesus established here and elsewhere. He never condoned waste, but rather taught against it (see Chapter V), but Judas had a false conception of waste. That which is given into God's service is never wasted. Rather, how may we be guilty of waste? One way is to misuse what we have, as the prodigal son did (Lk. 15:13). The word *prodigal* means *wasteful.* How did he waste? By wrongly using not only his possessions but his life, his time, his soul — everything! Another way to waste is by failing to use. The one-talent man wasted his talent, not by a corrupt use of it, but by a failure to use it at all — and this waste was called wickedness by Jesus (Matt. 25:24-30). The real waste would have been for Mary to keep the precious perfume, unused though she had a glorious once-in-a-lifetime opportunity for friendship, adoration, and thankfulness.

5. *Other disciples joined in the criticism,* not stopping to think for themselves, though evidently not moved by the same evil motives as Judas. How often people hear a disparaging remark about a fellow Christian and then join in the criticism, never stopping to realize that they are actually letting an evil mind do their thinking for them.

III. "SHE HATH DONE WHAT SHE COULD."

1. *Small things become great when dedicated to God.* All of us would like to be remembered favorably, by the Lord as well as posterity. Some think this requires great wealth to build massive church buildings or schools or hospitals. But this is not true. Mary's gift, though costly, was materially insignificant when compared with many of the world's great gifts. Who would think that anybody could ever become famous because of a mere bottle of perfume? She could not preach like Paul or lead great armies like David, but she did what she could.

A lunch is insignificant, but the boy who gave his to Christ gained a place in history (Jno. 6:9-11). A stone in the sling of the shepherd boy David was a small thing, but its impact is felt even until now (I Sam. 17:20).

A number of years ago, a five-year old boy said to his mother: "I want to do something for Jesus. I can't do much, but I want to ask all the people in our neighborhood to go to church with us. I'm not very good at talking. So I want you to write a note for me, and I'm going to all the houses and knock on the doors and ask the mothers to read the invitation." He did. Can you imagine the effect this had on the mothers contacted? So much that some of them accepted!

Could Christ say of us: "She hath done what she could"?

> Find out what God would have you do,
> And do that little well;
> For what is great and what is small
> 'Tis only he can tell.

IV. THE FAR-REACHING FRAGRANCE.

The power of influence is greater than any of us can realize. Surely Mary had no idea of the far-reaching effects of her simple deed, but she seized the opportunity while she could. Jesus pointed out two definite results. One involved world-wide influence. Countless memorials built to monarchs and noblemen have crumbled and sunk into silence — but the memorial to Mary is enshrined for all time, living and sparkling for each generation, ever new and fresh and lovely. The fragrance of the perfume filled not only the house in Bethany but spread throughout the world.

Another aspect of her influence involved Christ himself as the recipient. Baring the loneliness of his sorrow-laden heart, he said, "Against the day of my burying hath she kept this," alluding to the spices and ointments used by Jews to prepare the bodies of their dead. Though Christ had spoken of his impending death, his disciples did not fully comprehend it. In essence he is saying: "The effect of this gift is greater than any of you can understand." Her gift of love meant more to him than even Mary supposed — as all gifts of love do, if that love is shared. The gift is measured by the motive. If your child brings you wild daisies picked with his own little hands, or a crumpled picture drawn just for you, the gift's impact upon you is measured by the motive and means more to you than the child can possibly know.

Your influence is greater than you realize. No person lives or dies to himself. No person goes to heaven or hell alone. No matter who you are, your influence is woven forever into the fabric of other lives here and hereafter. Just one generation of women totally committed to Christ, as Mary was, could revolutionize the world and change the whole course of civilization.

V. YOUR ALABASTER BOX.

You have an alabaster box. Everyone does, though they come in various sizes and degrees of potency. What is your alabaster box? Everything you have within your power to bestow upon another. What is your most valuable possession? Your soul, of course. But what is the most precious gift which can be given to another? Your love — the affection, loyalty, and devotion of your heart. "And thou shalt love the Lord thy God with all thy heart, and with all thy soul and with all thy mind, and with all thy strength: this is the first commandment" (Mk. 12:30). This is total commitment! When the heart is given, all other gifts naturally follow: your wealth, your time, your talent, your body, your influence. These are all contained in your alabaster box, which, when given to the Master, send forth a lovely fragrance which tells Him and the world that He is the object of your affection. And it should be easy to love the Lord wholly, when we understand how much he loves us, as discussed in Chapter III. Mary's gift merely testified that she had already given her greatest treasure, her heart.

The choice is yours. Merely to possess some costly perfume would have meant nothing to Mary. Surely others had the same. The greatness came through its use. Today you possess an alabaster box. To possess it is no merit within itself. It is your use of it which will determine your happiness and destiny. Mary's gift required a willingness to give up something. She had to make a choice. She could have chosen to keep the luxurious perfume and use it on herself; but, if so, she would have forfeited the joy and honor which came from giving it. Every blessing is gained at the cost of giving up something else. The candle must shine at the expense of the wick. The choice is yours. You can keep all your treasures, lavish them upon yourself, and lose heaven. Or you can use them in God's service and thereby emit a fragrance so far-reaching that it will extend into eternity.

> Whatever dies, or is forgot —
> Work done for God, it dieth not.

Mary's challenge to us. Though we are not given a word spoken by Mary on this occasion, her deed speaks a forceful challenge today: "Will you also break your alabaster box? Will you give your best to the Master?"

> Were the whole realm of nature mine,
>   That were a present far too small;
> Love so amazing, so Divine,
>   Demands my life, my soul, my all.
>
> — Isaac Watts

REVIEW EXERCISE

1. List some of Mary's traits which are revealed by her gift to Christ. ....
....
....

2. What reason did Judas give for objecting to Mary's deed? ....
....

3. What was the real reason for his objection? ....
....

4. What did Christ say in defense of Mary? ....

....

....

5. What does the word "prodigal" mean? ....

6. How did the one-talent man waste his talent? ....

   What did Jesus call him? ....

7. (T or F) It is possible to keep something and by so doing to waste it.

8. What is the most precious gift which you can bestow upon another? ....

9. Name some things contained in your alabaster box. ....

....

FOR THOUGHT OR DISCUSSION

1. Think of some constructive things which could be done with the time we waste. For instance, could we read the entire Bible this year? Cheer the heart of many shut-ins? Convert a soul to Christ?

2. A young woman said: "The Bible says to love God with all the heart, but I want my husband to love me more than anything else." Who makes the best husband? One who loves God with all his heart, or one who doesn't? Who makes the best wife? One who loves God with all her heart, or one who doesn't? Why?

3. Some have said: "I would like to love God more, but how can I?" Consider again the reasons Mary loved Christ so. The same apply to us. Another way to increase appreciation of anything is to imagine what life would be without it. Think often of what our plight would be without God. We breathe his air, eat his food, live in his world, and depend upon him for the very life within us, as well as all spiritual blessings. If you would increase your love, sacrifice for the Lord's cause. We love those for whom we sacrifice. This is one reason you love your children.